Elizabeth TAYLOR

Elizabeth TAYLOR

TOM HUTCHINSON

Exeter Books

NEW YORK

Photographic acknowledgments

Camera Press, London 39 top; EMI Films 75 top; Keystone Press Agency, London 40; Kobal Collection, London 9 bottom, 10, 12, 14, 15, 17 top, 17 bottom, 19, 20 23, 24, 25, 26–27, 29, 30, 31 top, 31 bottom, 34, 35, 37, 39 bottom, 48, 49, 58, 59 bottom, 61 top, 63, 65, 68, 70 top, 73, 76; National Film Archive London 11, 13 top, 13 bottom, 16, 18, 21 top, 21 bottom, 22, 28 top, 32 top, 32 bottom, 33, 36, 42, 43, 45, 47 bottom, 52, 53, 56 bottom, 57, 60, 61 bottom, 62 top, 62 bottom, 66 top, 66 bottom, 67, 75 bottom; Photographers International, Chilworth, Surrey 78; Popperfoto, London 28 bottom, 38, 41, 59 top; Rex Features, London 8, 9 top, 46, 47 top, 51, 54, 55, 69, 74, 76–77; Syndication International, London 7, 44, 64, 70 bottom, 71, 72; Twentieth Century-Fox 56 top.

Camera Press – Norman Parkinson 79

Front cover: Hamlyn Group Picture Library.
Back cover: *Beau Brummell* (MGM). Kobal Collection.
Frontispiece: Kobal Collection.

ISBN 0–89673–137–5

Printed in Italy

CONTENTS

GIRL ON A HOT TIN ROOF

She swept into the Press conference, with all the assurance of a queen, surrounded by her usual retinue of 'courtiers,' the yes-men and yes-women to her commands. She is smaller than you think and, perhaps, the legs beneath that immaculately cut skirt are stubbier than might be classically correct. But her face is the fortune you collect by looking at her: a searchlight of beauty, with large, lustrous, violet eyes set in a symmetrically oval frame beneath that mass of blue-black hair.

She moved from cluster to cluster of journalists, bestowing answers to their questions, the males preening in her presence, the women looking rather diminished and faded by contrast. We asked her how many diamonds she had now and she couldn't remember, laughing a surprisingly raucous laugh. We asked her about future movies and she said she was always reading scripts but hadn't settled on one yet. Past films? She looked suddenly serious. 'I never look back: it's too painful.'

But hadn't she succeeded beyond the wildest dreams of many women? 'I never look back: it's too painful.' And, suddenly, embarrassingly, her eyes were full of tears, brimming but not overflowing. She signalled to one of her entourage and walked away rapidly and out through the door. The Press conference – a rare enough event with her, anyway – was over.

Thus, Elizabeth Taylor. Descending from Olympian heights, only to retreat back up there because of the pain that might be inflicted by the reality of memory: the bruising touch with her public. Back to the rarified dreams that money can buy, away from the stifling gasp of ordinary oxygen.

In herself, Elizabeth Taylor is surely the most remarkable human ambiguity in show business. Adored by millions she has been villified by as many. The most beautiful woman in the world? Yet, at the same time, she has been the sickest, her illnesses making headlines whenever she had to take to her bed. Described by the director Joseph M. Mankiewicz as the most loyal and least promiscuous actress he has met, she has been married seven times.

She is the most public of properties, yet the most private of persons. 'There is a point of privacy beyond which I simply will not go, because it would involve throwing mud,' she has said. Yet mud has been thrown at *her*. It never, in any way, stuck enough to mask her stardust.

For that stardust grew outwards from within, is a natural element of her personality: it is not imposed from without by the artificial methods of promotion or publicity. She exudes a glamour that is at once erotic and tranquil (another riddle). As Richard Burton, her one-time husband and partner with her in what became known as The Scandal, said: 'She brings repose.'

Yet what she brings herself are emotions by no means as peaceful as that. I was once told by a woman publicist, who was close to her, part of a group of retainers which at one time threatened crowd proportions: 'She has this outward, cool beauty. But inside she's a ferment of emotions, especially when she is preparing a script for a film. She takes the stories about herself very seriously. They can wound her. When she was beginning the love affair with Richard and a Vatican newspaper made that indirect attack upon her, she was near breakdown. She reached for anything: pills, drink, anything to numb what she felt of as hurt.'

This suggests that Elizabeth Taylor is a passive creature, a person to whom things are done rather than one who does. But, anyone who has survived as she has done within the jungle of show business and maintained an integrity of performance in doing so, is some kind of fighter: a prize kind of fighter. Anyone who has come through the number of illnesses she has had – from spinal operations through simple dislocations to breath-halting pneumonia – can swing an upper-cut at fate with the best of them.

I was once with her and Richard Burton in a bar in London's Hampstead village and he was ribbing her about her film fame, half-mockingly comparing it with his then considerable stage career. She took it for some time, then 'It might not be as prestigious as yours, Richard,' she said, with a

flash of smiling steel, 'but it's certainly helped to get you a larger salary.'

'Touché!' said Burton kissing her on the cheek.

For, to another writer he once said, 'Before I met Elizabeth I was making 175 thousand dollars a picture. Now I'm making half a million . . . it makes you think, doesn't it? If I retired tomorrow I'd be forgotten in five years, but she could go on for ever. She's a legend in her own lifetime.'

She is a legend who can give as good – or as bad – as she gets. At just under 5 feet 5 inches (1.65 m), she stands tall even among the greats of Hollywood. Yet it is a stature she has achieved with only a handful of good movies, films of any kind of artistic respectability. She has, as she once admitted, 'made some real clinkers.'

That must be par for the course with any actress. Not many of them, though, would be as honest as Elizabeth Taylor to admit it.

No matter how the camera catches her, there is no escaping the aura that surrounds Elizabeth Taylor's presence.

So, too, this assessment of her will be honest. It is what she would expect, after all. Aware only too well of the fickleness of a public to which she at once belongs and from which she is remote – aware of the worship as well as the strictures – the envy as much as the adoration – she once said: 'The only stability you can fall back on is the truth.'

And the truth is, of course, that at a time when more and more stars become anonymous between movies, retreating back into their familial shells, Elizabeth Taylor – whether she likes it or not – has lived a life in full view of the public limelight, tanned by its fervent glow. She may disdain its illumination, but she has been bronzed by it. And, implicitly, this is something she admits, when she once wrote about her early career in Hollywood: 'Every kid's dream is to be older, to dress up, to make believe. And to live in a world of fantasy.'

That is just what she did. That is what made her a superstar. That is what made her a queen of our time.

Elizabeth Rosemond Taylor was born on 27 February 1932, in a London hospital to Sara Taylor, wife of Francis Taylor, both of them Americans living in England, a fact which gave Elizabeth automatic dual citizenship. Father was an art dealer managing a gallery in London's Old Bond Street and their home, called Heathwood, was in Hampstead Village.

Sara had had some small acquaintanceship with the stage as an actress in repertory-stock in America, but she enthusiastically denied that she was that well-known mother-figure cliché from the movies – the one who pushes her daughter into a stage persona she herself has had to discard. Although it has to be admitted that she did take the young Elizabeth along to meet the famous gossip columnist Hedda Hopper, so that Elizabeth could show off her vocal prowess: singing for her Hopper rather than her supper. And it was Mama who coped with the tantrums of L. B. Mayer, the famed boss of MGM Studios, when Elizabeth was under contract there.

Certainly, Sara Taylor insists that 'I never looked back' after marrying Francis. The stage and all it stood for in the way of glamour and tinsel was just a faint regret in the past. Her major role now was bringing up a family, a family which Elizabeth was later to regard as the central pole around which the full tent of her personality was to unfold. That was her centre of gravity, her equilibrium for all the hectic years ahead.

She has an elder brother, Howard, who is nearly three years older than she is. She worshipped him with a kid sister's undying sense

Left: A triumphant Liz after her stage success in a revival of 'The Little Foxes' at the Martin Beck Theater in 1981. It was a strenuous role for her after illness.

The Taylors decided to return to America, which they did, leaving the pony and memories – for Elizabeth – that had included ballet classes which meant that she had once danced before the Duchess of York, soon to be Queen, and her daughters, Elizabeth and Margaret. Perhaps forebodings of show-business regality stirred within Elizabeth then: she was already, at seven, a child who would often dream the time away, a process which she later called – when she had read the James Thurber story – 'Walter Mittying.'

Reality, though, meant that her father set up an art gallery in Hollywood and the family was living in the Pacific Palisades. For Elizabeth it meant school. But it was school where the pupils were of an extraordinary kind – the sons and daughters of Hollywood personalities, whether it be producer or actor or director: a junior celebrity bulletin.

It was there that she met a boy called John Derek, soon to be a star, and had a crush on him. And it was there that she wanted to be an actress and, when the others laughed – they were blasé about it all, as who wouldn't be with their backgrounds? – insisted that her choice was to be a 'serious actress, like my mother was'.

It was, in fact, a time for child-stars. Shirley Temple was the prima donna in that direction, of course, while Deanna Durbin had sung one studio out of near-bankruptcy. Thus the vocal audition with Hedda Hopper.

that the adored one can do no wrong. She still does: 'He's my best friend of all and I trust him utterly. He is such a wise, tender, brilliant, different man.' She regards him as a non-conformist, but that may have been in his philosophy; certainly her own life-style has not conformed or succumbed to many things.

So her infant life in London was a happy one, although her first recollection of that time is of fierce pain. Baby-like, she crawled towards the glowing red electric fire that clung to the wall and poked a finger into the wires. Her wail was said to have been heard outside the house; her finger was nastily damaged.

Healing time was on her godfather's estate in Kent, although there were misadventures there, too, notably the gift of a pony called Betty that almost immediately threw her into a patch of stinging nettles. The antidote of nearby dock-leaves was quickly applied and Elizabeth resumed riding.

England itself seemed to be riding for a different kind of fall as, in 1939, the threat of Hitler and Nazi Germany massed into a monstrous nightmare. Most of Europe had been engulfed and Britain seemed to be next on the monstrous carnivore's menu.

Below: The 4½-year-old Liz on her first horse Daisy. She has retained a love of horses, and her riding ability helped her in her early success in the film *National Velvet*.

For singing moppets were the mostest about this time: perhaps it was that their innocence was such a box-office lure when balanced against the war clouds which even Isolationist America felt to be lowering on the other side of the Atlantic.

Due to a lucky acquaintance of her parents' Elizabeth got the chance of a screentest at MGM, managing to catch studio chief Louis B. Mayer, who with the catch-all instinct of scooping up any talent around was said to have shouted: 'Sign her up!'

The offer, when it came, was not so magnanimous as it might have been: 100 dollars a week for seven years, with yearly options. But somebody – may it not have been stage-wise Sara? – parlayed that into a chance to join the rival Universal Studios, who offered her 200 dollars a week, even though the casting director Dan Kelly said of her:

'The kid has nothing. Her eyes are too old. She doesn't have the face of a kid.' It was a judgement that he was never quite able to live down thereafter.

Elizabeth was then just around ten years old and found herself in a film called *Man or Mouse*, in which she had, as a juvenile partner, Alfalfa Switzer, whose previous claim to fame was in the *Our Gang* movies. *Man or Mouse* was retitled *There's One Born Every Minute*. Which didn't help it either. Elizabeth can hardly remember what it was about, but it was notable for containing three aged comedians, Hugh Herbert, Guy Kibbee and Edgar Kennedy.

That was the only film she made in her first year with Universal. As a token of its gratitude the studio, after that year, said she was no longer under contract and bade her a fond farewell.

As a child Elizabeth Taylor had stunning good looks, which altered so little that she is instantly recognizable even in this picture of her at the age of nine.

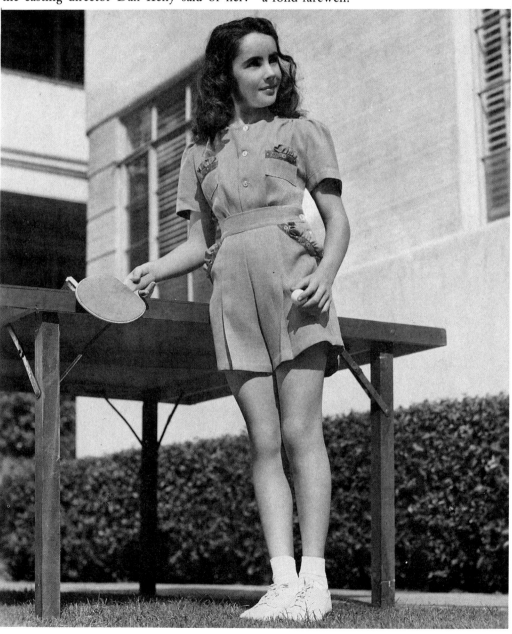

Elizabeth, however, was not inordinately grieved at this break: her inner ear had caught the sound of a distant music which seemed to suggest that her life might march to a different tune. It was the far-off, sweet sound of a dog barking. . .

The family had, by now, moved to Beverly Hills, where a friend of her father's was an MGM producer called Samuel Marx. Marx was readying, with director Fred M. Wilcox, a film which – had they known – was to become the first of a highly popular series: *Lassie Come Home*.

This was an account of canine devotion. The faithful collie Lassie, having been separated from her young master, Roddy McDowall, treks across half Britain to be with him again, coming across adventures, villains and animal lovers wherever she goes. Elizabeth went along for a screen test, 'Walter Mittying' herself into patting an invisible collie dog – and she was in the film as the young aristocrat who speeds Lassie on her way.

She was also, at a stroke (of the pen), within the sacred portals of MGM, whose

The 11-year-old in her first big success, with her co-star lying doggo, and the other actors struggling against the proverbial scene-stealers, a child and an animal. Liz in *Lassie Come Home* (MGM).

Left: Liz in a scene from *National Velvet* (MGM), her first big starring role. She and Mickey Rooney are trying to employ Eugene Loring, who is sceptical of the horse's chance.

boast that it had more stars than there were in heaven was going to be further validated by the inclusion of Elizabeth.

But that was to be in the future. She had made it into *Lassie Come Home* (a) on account of her English accent; (b) she seemed at ease in the studio; (c) she was petite (a previous girl had towered over Roddy McDowall, who was after all the hero). What might be called a case of England, Home and Cutie. . .

That English accent was to get her a small, uncredited role in *Jane Eyre* on loan to Twentieth Century-Fox. There she reverted to MGM again, this time for *The White Cliffs of Dover*, a sentimental weepie with Irene Dunne, which paid an affectionate tribute to a now at-war Britain, without actually going into battle on that country's behalf.

After that, Elizabeth went into battle on her own behalf. And the reason for that fight was another animal picture. It was to be the most important of her career so far and, talking only a few years ago, she was heard to say, 'I still think *Velvet* is the most exciting film I've ever done.'

The film's full title is *National Velvet*, from the best-seller written in 1935 by Enid Bagnold, about the butcher's young daughter, in an English country village, winning the Grand National Steeplechase on a horse called 'The Pi'. For a girl who was horse-mad, who could jump without a saddle at the age of three, it was a movie she felt made for her. She had to be in it; she was pi-eyed with ambition to be the girl in the story, Velvet Brown.

That mind can surmount matter is proved by the story of how Elizabeth got the part. She went along to see the producer, Pandro S. Berman, who measured her against a wall

with a pencil. It was no go. At the age of twelve, Elizabeth was only the height of a six-year-old. So sorry.

'Don't call us, we'll call you' is one of the worst sounds an actor or actress is likely to hear. Elizabeth decided to call Berman three months later. He measured her against that same wall – and she had grown 3 inches (8 cm). She got the role of Velvet Brown.

How had she achieved it? She had eaten two huge breakfasts every morning, besides her other plate-filling meals. Then she had indulged in strenuous swimming and other exercises. Just to help her grow that extra bit. Berman said, many years after: 'Elizabeth's will to win was really extraordinary.' With him, you might say, she had made her mark. She was about to make an even more indelible mark.

Above: A 12-year-old Liz providing some young calf-love interest in her fourth film, *The White Cliffs of Dover* (MGM), with Roddy McDowall.

Far left: The future star relaxing, and showing that at the age of around 12 she was just as much at home with an anonymous dachshund as with the famous collie she starred with.

FROM MAYER TO HILTON — AND BACK AGAIN

Far right: Dogs and horses featured prominently in the films and the publicity of the young actress. It says much for Liz that even such a handsome balancing trio as this cannot take all the attention from her.

The handsome King Charles was an aristocrat by breeding and bad-tempered by nature, but as 'The Pi' he helped Liz, Mickey Rooney and Jackie 'Butch' Jenkins make a great success of *National Velvet* (MGM).

The horse that was to play 'The Pi' was a handsome gelding called King Charles, who had been grandsired by the famous Man O' War. King Charles was a notorious steed, who had bitten his trainer and who had a reputation for throwing his riders. One wonders, therefore, why he was chosen to carry Elizabeth Taylor who, although an accomplished horsewoman, was then still only twelve – and vulnerable.

Even she admits, 'He really was a lunatic. Just for the hell of it he once jumped over an automobile.' But she always had a way with animals – her mother thought they ought to have a ranch instead of just a home, so many pets did she have – and King Charles followed his young mistress around rather like a dog who feels that there may be a bone hidden away in the pocket of her pants. Some of her male admirers were to feel the same slavish way, but they were to come later.

At the moment all she felt was platonic affection for and gratitude to a member of the opposite sex, Mickey Rooney, who nicknamed her Mona Lizzy. He confessed later that he never really understood her on this movie. At one point when 'The Pi' is sup-

posed to be close to death he gave Elizabeth some Method-style advice on how to shed real tears. But all she could do was burst out giggling. But she did it her way – and brought forth real tears.

As a film *National Velvet* could so easily have been a cliché of rural life, English as she is spoke in Hollywood terms, filled with Mummerset dialogue and stereotypes of the way English people are supposed to behave. Thankfully, it didn't work out like that. It had a sharpness of observation that saved it from being syrupy and its performances by all – including Donald Crisp as Velvet's father and Anne Revere as her mother – were fresh and attractive. It is still a movie to see.

Certainly, it was a film that saw Elizabeth Taylor become a star. Young as she was, she and the film were what people wanted to see: there was a brightness to the picture and to her: a luminosity that shone through her like a watermark. And when she was presented with King Charles on her thirteenth birthday she knew that she was being recognized as a star by the studio that had become the most famous in Hollywood.

Not even an appearance in an inevitable, and inferior *Lassie* follow-up, could daunt her realization that she was more than halfway to becoming a celebrity. *Courage of Lassie* was a plot-convoluted weepie about Lassie being recruited into the Army, after being separated from Elizabeth, becoming what is thought of as a killer-dog but redeeming himself just in time for the final credits.

Although it wasn't as good as *Lassie Come Home*, it was much better than the films that followed, in which the theme became, literally, dog-tired. Elizabeth, though, had said goodbye to animals as co-stars for a while. She and her mother wondered what she was going to do next.

What she did was unheard of, even if it was often contemplated at MGM, where the hierarchy was rigid. At the top of the status-pyramid was L. B. Mayer. Mayer was a tycoon very much of his time: a bully for all seasons who could weep when viewing a film of sentiment; a man who could tell his

A girl and her dog . . . and the most famous of all dogs. Liz and Lassie in a typical weepie about the misunderstood dog who always came good in the final reel, *Courage of Lassie* (MGM).

stars that he was a father to them, yet fire people without a moment's notice. He was part-hypocrite, part-charlatan, and in his way, part-genius.

And he had a temper which could flatten mountains. Elizabeth encountered it when she was only fourteen years old. And she pushed back.

The talk around the studio was that she was going to appear in a film to be called *Sally in Her Alley*. She and her mother managed to secure a meeting with Mayer to ask if it were true. The reason was that the heroine of the story would have to sing and dance – and Elizabeth would therefore have to start training.

For some reason nobody has ever been able to fathom, Mayer exploded. Obscenity after obscenity flowed from his lips like sewage from a pipe. 'You and your daughter,' he raged at Sara, 'are nothing. I took you from the gutter and I can put you back there!'

Elizabeth's temper could be an awesome thing of nature, too. Even at fourteen. She jumped to her feet and shouted: 'Don't you dare to speak to my mother like that! You and your studio can go to hell!' And she ran

sobbing from the room. She never ran back and, although advised to, she never apologized. The whole studio was aghast. Nobody spoke to Mayer that way! But somebody just had: a teenager called Elizabeth Taylor. Would she survive?

She survived all right, although years later she still talked of that experience with Mayer; it was her first experience of an ego made brutal by too much licence. Strangely, though, Mayer never did anything further about it, but perhaps that was because he was engaged in his own boardroom struggles. Anyway the heat was taken off Elizabeth for a while, because she was on loan-out once again, this time for five months on a film called *Life with Father*, a nostalgic turn-of-the-century piece for Warner Brothers.

It was a gentle piece of hokum, but Elizabeth was third down the billing, below Irene Dunne and William Powell: not a bad placing for a girl who was celebrating her fifteenth birthday. Fifteen, maybe, but she was filling out the frilly blouses and flouncy dresses of the film's period with ample charms. Michael Curtiz, the director of *Life with Father*, declared her to be 'the most promising ingenue in years.'

Promising or not, ample or not, she was now much more aware that she was of some value to MGM – that they could make money out of her – and not quite so star-struck as she used to be. There had been the time when she would blush simply because Clark Gable had come into the studio restaurant. But she didn't now. And she didn't ask anyone for autographs, ever since Katharine Hepburn had looked straight through her while signing the book that Elizabeth had so shyly proffered.

Adolescence is a tough time, anyway. For Elizabeth it was tougher because of school '. . . because it wasn't school . . . we were required by law to put in three hours a day, so we were doing in that time what normal kids did in six.' A tutor on the film set didn't help much either. It was the constant adjustment between being an actress and learning lessons that caused the mind-jolting difficulties.

Because the other film youngsters were in the same boat, there was no real time to build up any kind of lasting friendship. Besides there were only about six pupils at a time, all of different grades. She would listen to stories of the easygoing cameraderie at Howard's school with wide-eyed wonder and envy.

Meanwhile the films were being made, although they added little to Elizabeth's understanding of the art of which she was capable. There were such forgettables as *Cynthia*,

Above: Liz was billed below beautiful Irene Dunne and debonair William Powell in *Life with Father* (Warner Bros.), but at 15 years old her beauty was blossoming and more mature roles were imminent.

Left: Liz is well back in the procession to church led by William Powell and Irene Dunne in *Life with Father* (Warner Bros.).

in which she played an over-protected daughter, and *Julia Misbehaves*, which teamed her with Greer Garson as the mother who deserted her when small to take up a career on the music halls. Always the daughter, you see. But *Julia Misbehaves* was notable for her friendship with Peter Lawford, whom she considered a sophisticate among sophisticates.

She had her first screen kiss in *Cynthia*, and with Lawford it was something she looked forward to. She tells it: 'In the scene where he had to kiss me I was supposed to say, "Oh, Rock, what are we going to do?" After the kiss I looked at him, turned a hot scarlet and said, "Oh, Peter, what am I going to do?" And the whole company fell down laughing. That's another moment when you want the floor to open.' Crushes can, indeed, be very crushing.

Elizabeth was blossoming into lovely womanhood, so much so that it seemed quite natural that she would be the bride in *Father*

of the Bride*, a delightful comedy directed by Vincente Minnelli, which had Spencer Tracy as the father bemusedly and amusingly bemoaning his confused lot as preparations for the wedding of his daughter take over his house and his life.

The loving discipline of marriage was something also inherent within Elizabeth's nature. Years later she said, 'I had always had a very strict and proper upbringing – and absolutely necessary it was, living the existence I did. The irony is that the morality I learned at home required marriage. I couldn't just have an affair. So I got married all those times and now I'm accused of being a scarlet woman.'

But at that time, of course, she was scarcely tinted a light pink. Although the MGM publicity department did their best to shade it deeper. It was their job to suggest dates for its young stars, a practice which Elizabeth deeply resented. But, in any case, the wolves were baying. At 17 Elizabeth was

Liz was the bride in *Father of the Bride* (MGM). Father was Spencer Tracy, bemused and bewildered by the whole business of the forthcoming wedding, and the attendant problems Joan Bennett and Liz sprang on him.

One of the first men to be linked romantically with Liz was former All-American footballer Lt Glen Davis, seen with her at the Academy Award ceremony of 1949.

a highly delectable prize. Even Howard Hughes, the notorious billionaire-recluse paid court – once he bought two paintings from Francis Taylor and then took Elizabeth out for dinner. But the odds seemed to be on sportsman Glenn Davis, who was paying ardent attention. Nibbles, Elizabeth's pet chipmunk, no longer seemed to be enough in terms of affection.

The American public assumed from Press reports that Elizabeth was engaged to Davis, although the rapidity with which the two of them parted should have dispelled the idea. Socialite William D. Pawley, Jr., was next. Here there was an official engagement. This was soon broken.

So it looked to outsiders as though there had been two aborted engagements within an incredibly short time. Elizabeth's image as a fickle temptress seemed to have started here. The films with which she was involved around this time seemed to communicate something: the innocent Amy in *Little Women* gave way to the formidable wife in *Conspirator*, married to the Communist agent of Robert Taylor. The title *Quo Vadis?* might well seem to be applied to her.

Eventually it looked as though all were going to be well. She was only just 18 when Paramount Studios borrowed her for *A Place in the Sun*. It was there that she met the

visiting tycoon Conrad Nicholson Hilton Jr.

Hilton was the eldest son of hotel magnate Conrad Hilton, aged 23 and a vice-president of the Hilton network. He was socially desirable and eminently wealthy. The friendship burgeoned under much public attention. For the public had seized upon Elizabeth's personality with great avidity, regarding her now as much their property as they did any other promoted star. Fan magazines called her 'The Luckiest Girl in the World' while soldiers voted her 'The Most Glamorous Pin-Up'.

She was everyone's dream of romance and the talk was how Elizabeth Taylor, who had a background of Christian Science, could reconcile herself to the Roman Catholicism of Nicky Hilton. No question about it: Elizabeth could reconcile herself all right. Elizabeth was in love.

The marriage took place at The Church of the Good Shepherd in Beverly Hills, before a congregation of stars including Fred Astaire, Ginger Rogers and Greer Garson – enough star power to light up a couple of cities.

Elizabeth kept cool during the ceremony – while Nicky was sweating profusely – but afterwards had three glasses of champagne. She was nervous, but her first marriage was well under way. Then it went way under. As

Liz with a more sophisticated hairstyle than usual to play the wife of Communist agent Robert Taylor in her first romantic lead in *The Conspirator* (MGM).

she wrote later, 'The Honeymoon in Europe lasted two weeks. I should say the marriage lasted for two weeks.' It ended, miserably, in the divorce courts eight months later.

FINDING A PLACE IN THE SUN

'Extreme mental cruelty' was the divorce complaint that Elizabeth brought against Hilton; she wanted no alimony from him. It was the least charge she could bring and it seemed very flimsy when the most that she could tell the court was that he had 'insulted' her parents and herself. The fact, though, that she had lost 20 pounds in weight while in Europe must have itself weighed with the lawyers because she got her divorce.

The real reasons? Certainly, she has never amplified what she has told the court at that time and Hilton, during his lifetime, never commented at all. The heart can hide its answers very well.

But Elizabeth could not hide from herself that she was wondering what kind of actress she was becoming at MGM. The studio was putting her into some strange vehicles for her

talent – *The Big Hangover* with Van Johnson was the least of it – and she confided that she was 'lost under a morass of mediocrity. Not just the scripts. I was mediocre, too.'

Self-doubt can be the most destructive of elements to an actress. But belief in herself was soon to be restored by the release of *A Place in the Sun*, about a year after it had been made. Against the competition of Montgomery Clift and Shelley Winters, besides other remarkable professionals, Elizabeth proved she could act beyond any reasonable doubt. Once and for all she was not just a pretty face – although she was that, all right. Bitterly, though, she realized that it was at Paramount Studios that *A Place in the Sun* had been made. Would her home studio have had that much faith in her? She doubted it.

A Place in the Sun was taken from the famous novel 'An American Tragedy' which brought fame to its writer Theodore Dreiser when it was published in the mid-1920s as well as notoriety for the number of towns and cities which considered its story to be of such impurity that their libraries should not

Left and below: Two scenes from the 1949 production of *Little Women* (MGM), based on the famous sentimental novel by Louisa M. Alcott of young sisters growing up. It was a remake of a 1933 film, and Elizabeth Taylor played Amy, a role taken in the first production by Joan Bennett, who was later to star with Liz in *Father of the Bride*.

Liz being directed on the set of the comedy *The Big Hangover* (MGM) while co-star Van Johnson, who played a man allergic to alcohol, looks on.

22

contain it. In fact it is a story of the deepest kind of morality, carving into the flesh of American materialism with a story that was based on a real-life murder.

A young, poverty-stricken man had killed his factory-girl fiancée, who was pregnant by him, because she was a hindrance to his plans to wed a rich girl. This theme Dreiser developed until its resonances showed up the society in which the man found himself: a context of greed and avarice. An earlier film version had found extreme disfavour with Dreiser, but the version that had been prepared by director George Stevens would overcome these objections.

Montgomery Clift played the young killer, Shelly Winters the doomed fiancée and Elizabeth the rich girl. It was to be a film in which she was to find her own place in the sun. Stevens said about the novel that 'its greatness lies in the fact that it is all things to all people. . . we'll try to tell it easily and honestly, without dramatic contrivances.'

Dramatic contrivances, though, there were: necessarily so. And performances of some magnitude. And it is against these that Elizabeth's must be measured. As the rich girl falling in love with a man below her class she could have portrayed the woman as a vacuous nonentity spoiled by her background. But she comes through in *A Place in the Sun* as a complex personality of some depth. 'I think she was a girl who could care a great deal,' said Elizabeth. That and more is what she put into the role.

It helped, too, to be working with Montgomery Clift, whom she had first met when she had been studio-dated by him to go to the premiere of his *The Heiress*. All she remembers of that evening is that Clift huddled up in his seat, as the dramatization of a Henry James story unfolded, muttering: 'Oh, my God, it's awful.' Elizabeth was always attracted to people and animals who seemed even more vulnerable than she, and Clift had an extremely complex personal life.

The real-life bride leaving the Church of the Good Shepherd in Beverly Hills after her wedding to Nicky Hilton. After a honeymoon in Europe, Liz went back to films, Hilton to running the Bel Air Hotel, and the marriage lasted only eight months.

The garlanded Elizabeth Taylor and Montgomery Clift each won plaudits for their performances in *A Place in the Sun* (Paramount), a film which won many Oscars, but not for Liz or Clift.

He took it out on himself via booze and drugs and Marilyn Monroe said of him, 'He's the only person I know who's in worse shape than I am.' Elizabeth just had to love him.

Loving friends they were, and that is how it was always to remain, even though she did regard him as 'the most gorgeous thing in the world and easily one of the best actors.' Such admiration did not blind her, either, to the fact that Clift's method of concentrating on his role was of immense importance to him — and to the film. Despite constant arguments with director Stevens he had pulled off a tremendous feat of acting.

Elizabeth's own acting thrived by imitation in this case and the critics were well-nigh universal in their acclaim of her when the film opened. An Oscar went to George Stevens for best director that year of 1951; if it were not for the competition of such movies as *A Streetcar Named Desire* and *An American in Paris* and the acting involved there, Elizabeth might well have got her first Oscar. That was to come in the future.

At the time the praise seems to have been enough. It helped heal the wounds made by the Hilton marriage and helped her to forget the brief relationship she had with a young

MGM director called Stanley Donen. Sara Taylor once told an interviewer: 'Elizabeth always had a very strong mind of her own.' That might be so, but such strength as she had might well have been broken by the public displeasure of her two broken 'engagements' and that broken marriage. *A Place in the Sun* helped rehabilitate her image, of which she had to be conscious if she were to continue in her chosen career as film star. A trip to the country of her birth might well help the healing process.

The journey to England was to make *Ivanhoe*, a medieval pageant also starring Robert Taylor, adapted from the novel by Sir Walter Scott. It was a Hollywooden enough movie, but director Richard Thorpe gave it a lot of momentum and Elizabeth's performance as the Jewish girl, Rebecca, who conceives a hopeless passion for Ivanhoe has a touch of truth that is remembered long after the battles and jousts.

It was a difficult film for her to make: a possible ulcer was giving her a lot of pain and she was reduced to eating what she described as 'baby food'. To an interviewer at the time she said: 'My neck is killing me. Every morning at six o'clock they tape me into a wig that weighs two pounds. It's full

Elizabeth Taylor much admired Montgomery Clift. Here she is fixing his bow-tie before the premiere of *The Heiress*, in which he co-starred with Olivia de Havilland.

Liz was 20 years old in 1952
and now married to Michael
Wilding. After all the teen-age
films, MGM, who had
recently re-signed her, were
beginning to release publicity
shots of her in conventional
film star poses, displaying her
charms before a swimming
pool.

of pins that stick into me all day long. By
night I really have a neck-ache – and a
head-ache.'

Perhaps it is no wonder that she was later
to denigrate it as a 'medieval Western' and
a 'cachou'. It is more than that to those on
the outside, but she was on the inside: and
that's how it seemed to her.

Like it or not, it is a film which remains
high in the Taylor canon, because it was the
movie in which she re-established relations
with the man who was to be her second
husband; Michael Wilding, whose easy manners and gentle charm seemed to eliminate
the uneasiness he felt then, and was to feel
even more later, at being 20 years older than
Elizabeth.

They had first met while Elizabeth was
making *Conspirator* at MGM. He recalled
afterwards: 'When I first met her I wondered
why a girl so beautiful felt she needed all that
make-up.' She had layered it on, she admitted later, because she wanted to impress him.
The make-up was more discreet now, on this
re-meeting, and their friendship flowered
again – this time into love.

Wilding's career and success was based on
roles of the foppish kind that the British
public adores. He had made his name as a
light comedian of some distinction, with all
the manners of a gentleman and a light-
hearted approach to life apparent in his ca-
ressingly so-British voice. He had partici-
pated in some dramatic movies, but his real
fame came with appearances opposite Anna
Neagle in snob comedies that were often in-
ane, but also quite entertaining: *Spring in
Park Lane* and *Maytime in Mayfair* are titles
whose very nature sums up what they were
about. After the oppressive imprisonment –
and equality – of wartime the British yearned
for escapism back to the class structure
which had in-debt dukes falling for flower-
girls and singing merry little songs before
true love finds a way.

That suede-suave manner was not just
confined to those frolics; it carried through
into his real life. No wonder Elizabeth was
bowled over. 'He's one of the nicest people
I've ever known,' she said long after their
marriage was over. And it is typical of the
deference he showed to her and their relationship that she has always insisted that it
was she who asked him to marry her.

The wedding took place in London on 21
February 1952. The honeymoon took place
in a hotel in the French Alps. Said Wilding,
'We were both of us very high on each other
and the scenery helped. We did drink rather
a lot of champagne I remember.'

It seemed singularly appropriate that the
first film for Elizabeth after re-signing her
now-expired contract with MGM should be

Right: Fernando Lamas was Liz's co-star in her first film under her new contract with MGM, *The Girl Who Had Everything*. She also teamed up again with William Powell (centre).

Far right: Robert Taylor, Joan Fontaine and Elizabeth Taylor in the medieval costume drama *Ivanhoe* (MGM), in which Liz came to England to play a Jewish girl, Rebecca.

Below: The newly-weds. Elizabeth Taylor married the debonair English actor Michael Wilding in 1952. The cosy domesticity of the scene in their flat hides financial wrangles they experienced with MGM.

The Girl Who Had Everything. But appropriateness was about all the film had going for it. A remake of an earlier movie called *A Free Soul*, it was about a father-daughter relationship that eventually ends up at a murder trial. It was one of a series of films which had been so badly chosen for her by MGM that it seemed as though the studio were trying to get back at her for becoming a star. Perhaps the go-to-hell incident with Mayer had not been entirely forgotten. No wonder she later said about those films that 'I blank out when thinking of them.'

Not only that, but MGM, after weeks of pleading with her to re-sign with the studio, put her on suspension because she was having a baby. She and Wilding put themselves further in debt to MGM by borrowing from the studio: money for their house and for other expenses that would accrue from the baby.

That suspension was felt by Elizabeth to be a vast act of betrayal, which she never forgot. She also never forgot about going to see a studio executive for a loan. She was humiliated beyond measure, told that she 'hadn't planned things very well'. Later in her career, when she would haggle over contracts to the point when even lawyers would beg for mercy, she would murmur to herself that this was the reason: the humiliation.

But such grievances apart there was much to look forward to. And the item which the Wildings had anticipated most happily arrived on 6 January 1953. He was called Michael Howard Wilding.

ILLNESS, ACCIDENT AND TRAGEDY

The love-hate relationship that MGM had with Elizabeth continued and the bad scripts kept coming in. Among these was *All the Brothers Were Valiant* which was a travesty about two brothers who go down to the seas as whalers and who both love the same woman. That woman, thought MGM – after the suspension was over and the younger Wilding through the earlier traumas of life, – should have been a grateful Elizabeth. It wasn't to be. Elizabeth seemed to have gained a new strength from motherhood (after all, that was something a male studio executive couldn't achieve) and she said 'no'

Liz replaced Vivien Leigh in *Elephant Walk* (Paramount) opposite Peter Finch (right). The two stars were visited on set by Michael Wilding.

very loudly. Came another suspension. And bewildered angry looks from MGM officials. Didn't the girl realize they were doing her a favour?

One opportunity presented itself, but foundered on the rocks of getting it all together: that was for Elizabeth and Cary Grant to star in *Roman Holiday*, the film which was to bring fame and Oscar-fortune to Audrey Hepburn. Nothing came of it for Elizabeth. Then Paramount reared its snow-capped head once more. They were in trouble and needed help on their film *Elephant Walk*, now on location in Ceylon.

This was to be the film which impelled Peter Finch to the top, as a tea-planter taking his new bride to the jungle interior, there to meet manager Dana Andrews and sundry perils of which bull-elephants seemed the least. But the production was imperilled because Vivien Leigh, who was portraying the new bride, had had a nervous breakdown and had to be flown back to London and her husband, Laurence Olivier. What could be salvaged of the movie would be salvaged, but Elizabeth was needed to take up the role of the bride: perhaps a few long-shots of Vivien Leigh could stand in as photographed: the rest would have to be re-shot.

So, out to Ceylon went Elizabeth and the film was finally cobbled together with her help. However such an act of aid was not to be rewarded with the kind of gratitude that fate should have had in store. And, despite all the perils that could have befallen her in Ceylon, it was back in Hollywood, at Paramount Studios, that the real injury occurred.

She and Finch and Dana Andrews were sitting in a jeep with a wind machine whirring away at them. This was for some publicity stills which were to be taken of them for use in posters: to pump up the tension for a public that had no idea why elephants walk and probably couldn't have cared less if they had known. Then – something tiny, but vicious, hit her in the right eyeball.

Later she wrote: 'When the eye got goopy and stuff was coming out, I went to a doctor who probed around and said, "My dear, you have a foreign object in your eye." And I

Left: A publicity still issued by Paramount prior to the release of *Elephant Walk*.

Below: Peter Finch struggles to remove Elizabeth Taylor from the path of the elephants who 'walked' through everything, including their fine mansion, in the climax of *Elephant Walk* (Paramount).

said, "Anybody I know?" ' It was the kind of brave joke that was certainly needed later on because the foreign object had rusted in the eyeball and there had to be an operation. It was an operation without anaesthetic, because the patient's cooperation was needed in moving the eyeball around. 'They have a needle with a tiny knife at the end and you can hear them cutting your eye. It sounds rather like eating watermelon on a minor scale.'

A few days after this ordeal she went along to the doctor to have the bandages removed. The doctor's reaction was one of alarm and despondency, which was not the sort of reaction to bring solace to a patient who had been wondering is she were going blind. 'Oh, my God!' said the doctor. What had happened was that the eye had ulcerated.

Right: Liz watches in alarm as a difference between Roger Moore and Van Johnson looks like developing into blows in *The Last Time I Saw Paris* (MGM)

Rhapsody for strings. Liz might have thought it a bit too much of a fiddle as she was serenaded by Vittorio Gassman and others in *Rhapsody* (MGM).

Another operation was needed; it might, in fact, make the eye sightless. They wouldn't know until healing had begun and the further bandages were shed.

Elizabeth took a deep breath and said that they could go ahead. After all, as she said, what else could she do? She was left without options. So the operation took place, and afterwards she lay in a hospital bed in total darkness, because they had to bandage both eyes.

To keep up her spirits she played a game with herself, figuring out where everything was: the water glass, the radio, the make-up and all the other paraphernalia of glamour that she had to have near her to make her feel normal. She was proudly demonstrating these skills for Wilding when he came on a visit. She swept her hand to the side – and knocked a bottle of perfume to the floor. For the first time during this torment, she wept.

When the eventual time came to remove those bandages – in a darkened room lit only by a small night light – the doctors peered and probed and said 'look this way' and 'look that way.' Such ritual words, though, seemed to have worked their spell, because the eye was pronounced as fit, although her vision would be a little blurred for a day or two. After that it was back to work for MGM again and into one of those movies about which she said, in a manner that indicates that her eyesight was still very acute: 'A lot of those films around at that time I haven't seen, but I must have been appalling in them.' Critics at the time, though, commended her for her yeoman-like ability to cope with some dreadful lines; it was the vehicles that were wrong, not the passenger.

This new film was *Rhapsody* and Elizabeth was the spoiled little rich and bitch girl whose love of classical music is made more than physically manifest when she falls for violinist Vittoria Gassman, much to the

Stewart Granger as Beau
Brummell and Elizabeth
Taylor as Lady Patricia flirting
together in the 1954 Royal
Command Performance film
Beau Brummell (MGM).

alarm of father Louis Calhern. All works out
well in some way or another, for the girl
eventually goes off with pianist John Ericson. Paced forte instead of pianissimo it
might have become a rip-roaring emotional
drama of the kind which is all too easy to
ridicule but which does, indeed, grip at the
time.

Rhapsody was not gripping by any manner
of means, although it had a modest box-
office success. Elizabeth, however, wanted
more than commercial acclaim; she wanted,
indeed needed, a movie which would stretch
her, accommodate those talents which she
knew she possessed – had proved she possessed. Her next film, *Beau Brummell* was
not to be that film. No wonder Elizabeth –
perhaps pyschosomatically – was complain-
ing of ever-increasing back pains.

The real-life Beau Brummell was an 18th
century English fop who greatly influenced

the style of his times. He was played rather
woodenly by Stewart Granger, and Elizabeth was Lady Patricia, in a blonde wig no
less, who flirts and dallies with him. It was
chosen for the 1954 Royal Film Performance
in London and was promptly savaged by
British critics who saw its over-dressed mis-
understanding of the period as somewhat in-
sulting to the Royal Family that had to sit
through it all. Naturally, no royal comment
was available.

Her next film, *The Last Time I Saw Paris*,
was not all that much better, but it certainly
got better reviews, some small consolation
for having made four films in just under a
year. But consideration of that quartet would
have to await awhile for a cool analysis from
her. Her most immediate concern was the
fact that she was pregnant again. And Christopher Edward Wilding was born, via Cae-
sarean section on 27 February 1955 –

GRAUMAN'S CHINESE THEATRE

Proudly Announces

FOOT PRINT
CEREMONIES
WED. EVE. SEPT. 26
8:30 O'CLOCK
HONORING
ELIZABETH TAYLOR
ROCK HUDSON
AND PRODUCER-DIRECTOR
GEORGE STEVENS

One of the things the stars are expected to do. Rock Hudson and Liz put their foot and hand prints in the courtyard of Grauman's Chinese Theater, an old Hollywood custom.

Elizabeth's birthday, a day now doubly to be remembered.

Her career continued after maternal claims on her had slackened, and her next film was *Giant* for Warners and for director George Stevens, who had guided her so successfully in *A Place in the Sun*. Both had come a long way since then – Stevens had made *Shane* among others – but the reunion was not as happy as might have been expected. Even her co-star, James Dean, a young man of legendary cool, began to chafe at the pressures which began to seem intolerable as the production of *Giant* moved on remorselessly.

The film was adapted from a block-busting book by Edna Ferber, which portrayed Texas and its inhabitants as the larger-than-

life characters they are generally supposed to be. The action takes place over a span of years and Elizabeth had to age, if not gracefully, at least realistically.

It seems all too apparent that Stevens still thought of Elizabeth as the young girl who had been so biddable in *A Place in the Sun*. But she had found her own place since then. He was constantly criticizing her: for wanting to look glamorous, of not turning up on time on the set. Another co-star, Rock Hudson, says: 'It was as though he were wanting to needle Elizabeth all the time. Not that she was the only target. Jimmy Dean got a lot of flak as well.'

Shooting the film became, in her word, 'murderous'. She admired Stevens, but she never wanted to work with him again after the experience of *Giant*. Years later, she recalled, he asked her to play Mary Magdalene in a film he was making. She declined, pointing out that the last time was something she did cherish fondly in memory. 'I always thought we got along very well together,' said Stevens. And they *did* work together.

Perhaps typical of their relationship was that it was towards the end of shooting *Giant* that the devastating news came that Dean had been killed in a car crash in the Porsche which he drove at a rocket-like rate. Despite her obvious grief she had to report next day for the filming of her final scene.

Not surprisingly, and perhaps as a reaction to all this, Elizabeth was taken to hospital for two weeks with a twisted colon. It was not the only thing that was twisted in her life. Her marriage to Michael Wilding was corkscrewing to destruction, and then there was the accident that befell another, even closer friend than Dean: Montgomery Clift.

He and actor Kevin McCarthy had been to a small dinner party at the Wildings'; it was over at about 10:30 and the guests departed. Suddenly the Wildings were aware that McCarthy had returned and was standing white as a ghost, mumbling, 'My God,

With Rock Hudson again in the ambitious blockbuster *Giant* (Warner Bros.). It was not a happy film for Liz, who was constantly at odds with director George Stevens.

oh God, Monty's dead.' He wasn't, but he was so severely damaged in a car-crash about a block away that when Elizabeth arrived at the scene she remembers it in mercilessly vivid detail: 'I crawled into the car and lifted him away from the steering wheel. I found that he was breathing and moaning. All my revulsion about blood absolutely left me. I held his head and he started coming to. You could see his face. It was like pulp. He was suffering terribly from shock, but he was absolutely lucid. There was a tooth hanging on his lip by a few shreds of flesh, and he asked me to pull it off because it was cutting his tongue. . .'

Clift survived and plastic surgery made good much of the bad that had been done to his face. During his lifetime Elizabeth wrote: 'He is still a beautiful man. He is beautiful inside. I think his looks are even more poignant now because they are not so perfect.'

Also less than perfect was the Wildings' marriage: that twenty-year chasm in ages was a generation gap that was widening irrevoc-

Giant (Warner Bros.) was the last film in the short career of the legendary James Dean, who was killed in a car crash near the end of shooting. Despite her grief, Liz had to film the next day.

At a time in her life when tragedy haunted Liz, her great friend Montgomery Clift was badly injured in a car crash when leaving her after a visit, and Liz comforted him in the wreck.

ably, with Elizabeth feeling herself to be treated more and more as a daughter and less and less as a wife. Or was it not daughter, but sister? When they first married it was quite clear that Elizabeth was still very much in awe of Wilding and his impeccable manners, his air of cultivated breeding. At parties, she admitted later, she would go around asking: 'Where's Michael?' As a personality she only seemed to exist in his context. But that had changed, a process which had come about because of her growing maturity: because she now realized herself as an individual and an artist in her own right. Humphrey Bogart had told her to 'assert herself.' This was happening more and more now and their two sons, she says, were beginning to realize something was wrong.

It was about this time that she was considering the script for a film called *Raintree County*, which had been scripted from a best-selling book and was to be with Montgomery Clift. Wilding had career problems

of his own. She recalled: 'After five years my marriage with Michael Wilding had become the relationship for which we were much more suited – brother and sister. He's one of the nicest people I've ever known. But I'm afraid in those last few years I gave him rather a rough time, sort of henpecked him and probably wasn't mature enough for him.'

So, on 20 July 1956 the news of their separation was headlines in all the papers. Next day there was a phone call from a man she had met intermittently over the years. He had been pointed out to her in the MGM restaurant as one of the most dynamic of all the movie producers of the day. She and Wilding had had dinner with him. There had been an attraction, what she calls 'a tingle,' but nothing had come of it. After all, why should anything? She was happily married to Michael Wilding. Now. . .

'It's Mr Mike Todd on the phone,' said her secretary.

'MRS WILDING,
MEET MIKE TODD'

Mike Todd smoked giant cigars as though there were no tomorrow, perhaps suspecting that for him there might not be. In 1956 he was 49 and had packed a Barnum-sized capacity for hard work and showmanship into that life. Born in Minneapolis, named Avrom Goldbogen, he was a compulsive gambler who first came to attention at the 1933 Chicago World's Fair where he produced a 'Flame Dance' – which really was no more than a strip-tease but presented in a classy, elaborate manner.

Mike Todd in the Dorchester Hotel, London, in January 1957. When asked if he intended to marry Elizabeth Taylor he said: 'I can't hear you. I guess you'll have to shout.'

He first went bankrupt when he was 19, but was soon zinging back in the business, producing shows on Broadway with a Damon Runyonesque vigour which might have made him seem vulgar but for the fact that he had a self-taught erudition which could floor many people who were expecting somebody to patronize. He had been married twice – his first wife died, the second, the actress Joan Blondell, divorced him – and he had been trying to recoup money from a not very successful stage verion of the Jules Verne novel, 'Around the World in Eighty Days'.

So when Elizabeth took that phone call from him she certainly knew who he was – but not what kind of man he was. That was to come later. What he said on the phone was 'I have to see you right away.'

She met him in an executive office at an MGM which was becoming more and more deserted as the company's troubles grew and he almost frog-marched her into another less-public office, put her on a couch and pulled up a chair. He then embarked on a line of chat which, he admitted later, was 'one of the hardest bits of persuasion I've ever been involved in.' In effect he said that he loved her and that he was going to wed her. In more earthy jargon, the message was: 'Don't horse around. You're going to marry me.'

She remembers that she was transfixed by the man's eyes, and that she walked out of the office 'as in a trance'. He recalled that she gave him a smile which was 'disdainful'. Either way he had made some impact, for she wrote later: 'I ran away from Mike – a couple of thousand miles away.'

She left for Danville, Kentucky, to make *Raintree County*. It was a role which she did to some sort of silly perfection, making bricks for a character out of an idea which didn't have much straw. She played a schizophrenic Southern belle – of the *Gone with the Wind* variety – who tricks Clift into marrying her and goes wildly mad. It was a lush period piece which, when it was released, didn't go down very well at all. Perhaps it was Montgomery Clift who put his finger on

Left: When Liz was separated from Michael Wilding, the 49-year-old Mike Todd was frequently seen about with her as a close companion.

Below: Liz as a Southern belle in *Raintree Country* (MGM) opposite Montgomery Clift, whose accident occurred during the shooting of the film. Todd constantly phoned her on location.

Above: Liz and Todd had married by the time of the London premiere of *Around the World in 80 Days* at the Astoria in July 1957. Liz wore a ruby red chiffon gown by Dior.

Right: So little time together. Liz, Mike and baby Liza.

sassy, brash exterior there was a sensitivity that had no correspondence with the urgent, boisterous image he was always communicating. Another kind of communication between them was inevitable and necessary for her to know him better and deeper.

She got two weeks holiday from the location shooting and flew to New York in a special plane that Todd has sent for her. First sight was sufficient. They flew into each other's arms. There was no other proposal of marriage after that first preremptory command. There was no need. They knew that marriage was as predictable as the rising of the sun. Until divorce they had to be together. They were.

And, on the night of 17 October, they were together in New York for the world premiere of *Around the World in 80 Days*, 13 days after the newspapers announced that Elizabeth was finally asking for a divorce. Todd was personally at the sound controls in the cinema for the film that would win him an Oscar, the award of the New York Film Critics' Circle and the laurel wreath of the National Board of Review. This version of Jules Verne's book about Phineas Fogg, in Victorian England, betting his fellow clubmen that he can travel around the world in the title's time had just about every star in Hollywood – and the British theatre.

Todd had thrown party after party to promote his film: whether at Madison Square Garden in New York or the Battersea Pleasure Gardens in London, money was spent in profusion: and, of course, the amount of money spent was bally-hooed out of all proportion and into the kind of wild stratosphere in which Todd found himself so very much at home. It was for him and for Elizabeth a time of great excitement – an excitement which Todd seemed to be able to self-generate.

But that excitement was considerably deflated before their marriage. They had been to Nassau to visit the Press tycoon, Lord Beaverbrook, and were on a houseboat. The boat lunged to one side and Elizabeth, who had been walking down a stairway, fell about six steps – straight on to the base of her spine.

The pain was excruciating, but Elizabeth said that a chiropractor could slip it all back in place – if there was a place to slot it all into. Todd, however, was sternly insistent. In New York he insisted she went to the Presbyterian Hospital for X-rays. She submitted, partly because she liked being bossed around by him and also because she was aware that something was wrong with her right leg, which felt numbed. Besides 'I didn't care much whether I ever worked again or not and you know if you lose one

why. His accident had happened while he was making the movie and he said: 'The audience spends too much time trying to figure out which scenes were after my accident.' Altogether a disappointment, although reviewers were generally in accord that Elizabeth was very good in it. 'Dominating' was the least of the descriptions of her performance.

Disappointing the film may have been, but it was a memorable occasion for Elizabeth, because it was while she was making it that she really got to know Mike Todd – by telephone. He wooed her by wire and by flowers, and she discovered that beneath his

leg you've got another and you've got you're life.'

The operation cut all the dead bone in the spine – three discs were gone – and then pieces of bone from her hip and pelvis, and from a bone-bank, were made into bony 'match-sticks' that finally calcified and became a column about 6 inches (15 cm) long. She was paralyzed for a time, but the painful part was still to come: to keep the bone from sagging they had to rotate her with sheets. 'I felt like a pig on a spit,' she said. She would pass out with the agony, hearing somebody screaming and realizing that it was her own voice that she was hearing.

Mike Todd once said: 'To be a really great star you have to have an enormous amount of courage; you're walking a tightrope all the time and that takes a hell of a lot of guts. That's why Elizabeth is a great star. That's why she will always be a great star.' It was a quotation that she may have considered somewhat wryly while in hospital. But, either way, it was true. Her courage was being tested – and, despite everything, was standing the strain.

But all the bad things, like the good, come to an end. Everything seemed to be knitting into place and, after a period of convalescence, she was allowed to resume life away from hospital. There was another very good reason for her to get well and to leave medical care: marriage. That took place on 2 February after the divorce from Michael Wilding had come through. She and Mike Todd were finally hitched in Acapulco, and the gaudy splendour and excitement of the wedding was perhaps symbolic of all that their life together would be.

She has written: 'Our life together was not all lavish. We had some remarkably simple times – barbecues with the children, taking care of the house ourselves – no servants – going to bed early, reading, getting up early. We didn't go out every night – maybe out to dinner once or twice a week.'

But those times were really the exceptions. Theirs was a progress that was as much fêted and celebrated by the media as that of royalty. It seemed only right and proper and in keeping with the public's interest in them that Elizabeth should announce that she was pregnant. That sort of thing just had to keep you in the public eye.

But, because of that spinal structure, medical counsel at first suggested abortion. Elizabeth dug in her heels and a compromise was reached: elastic gussets were attached to the spinal brace she still wore. That way there would be adequate support.

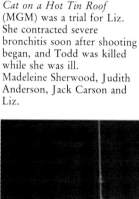

Cat on a Hot Tin Roof (MGM) was a trial for Liz. She contracted severe bronchitis soon after shooting began, and Todd was killed while she was ill. Madeleine Sherwood, Judith Anderson, Jack Carson and Liz.

In *Cat on a Hot Tin Roof* (MGM), Liz played the sexually frustrated wife of a crazy mixed-up cripple played by Paul Newman.

The baby was a girl – Elizabeth Frances Todd – and it was born, vastly premature, on 6 August. She weighed four pounds and four ounces and it took fourteen and a half minutes to get the child breathing. Elizabeth was overwhelmed with delight. She had known it would be a girl: 'There couldn't be two Mike Todds.' Todd, as always, had an appropriate thought for everything. He it was who had sent X-rays of Elizabeth's back to George Stevens, who had often said her pains were imaginary. Now, he already had a small gold hairbrush for Liza. He had known, along with Elizabeth, that the child was going to be a girl.

Both Elizabeth and Todd were considering other films. Todd was in the throes of preparing *Don Quixote* while Elizabeth was looking at the script of *Cat on a Hot Tin Roof* by Tennessee Williams – and deciding that this was to be her next movie. In between they managed to make headlines, their quotes always inspiring fascination.

MGM were up to their old tricks again; but they thought they knew what was best for her to make as a film. She wanted *Cat*. If they suspended her, she put it about, she could always retire early. She was strong enough within herself to do that now. So *Cat on a Hot Tin Roof*, with Paul Newman and Burl Ives as Big Daddy, began production in March. But after a fortnight Elizabeth contracted severe bronchitis and had to be confined to bed. She fought against it because she wanted to fly with Todd to New York, where he was to receive his award as Showman of the Year. She would have liked to share his joy in that honour, but illness soared her temperature to 102 degrees; it was imperative that she stay. He was to fly to New York in a private plane, but through some of the worst weather Southern California had known for a long, long time. He would ring her at various stops on the route.

But no phone calls came. Which was strange. Elizabeth wrote later that she was

43

Liz and Mike Todd a couple of months before he died. They were at the Dorchester Hotel in London before flying off for a visit to Moscow.

filled with foreboding; she asked the children's nurse for an alcohol rub as she was so hot. She lay awake through the night considering the excitement with which her life had been filled since meeting Mike Todd, how he had come back to kiss her six times on this departing – even though he would only be away for a short time.

Then at 8:30 in the morning, after that sleepless night, she was aware that the door had opened and there was a group of close friends. She knew instinctively and immediately what they were there for and she screamed out 'No!' But they nodded their heads: 'Yes!' She tried to run out into the street, clad only in her nightgown. They caught her and gave her a sedative. The truth sank into her consciousness like acid.

Mike Todd's plane had crashed, probably because of wing-icing, high up in the Zuni mountains of New Mexico, scattering its debris over 200 square yards. What remained of the bodies was identified later by dental charts and mementoes, such as Todd's gold wedding ring which was brought to Liz.

Elizabeth Taylor, superstar, was alone again. True she had her children, but that companionship which had become so important to her had been shorn from her. Joseph L. Mankiewicz, who was later to direct Elizabeth, wrote later: 'More than anyone realizes, Mike Todd was responsible for the intellectual and emotional awakening of this girl. For all his flamboyance, he was a man of an infinite variety of interests. Through him, Elizabeth became the step-grandmother of three children. She also travelled widely, meeting world statesmen and artists, swindlers and scientists, bankers and racket chiefs. Before that, she had been a sort of Sleeping Beauty in an isolated castle. Mike took her through the cobwebs to the outer world, in which there is something more than movie producers and wardrobe women. Before Todd, the people she knew outside the motion picture industry could probably be counted on the fingers of one hand.'

Elizabeth Taylor and Mike Todd had been extremely happy, in a marriage that lasted for just about 13 months.

A FISHER OF MEN

Mike Todd's funeral in Chicago was an ordeal which many, afterwards, likened to a similar scene in *A Star Is Born*, when fans swarmed all over the bereaved widow as though for some macabre premiere. The public appetite for celebrity could be a fearsome, frightening thing. The streets approaching the cemetery were thronged and Elizabeth, wearing a black hat with a small black veil, remembers hearing some girls crying out, 'Oh, dig that crazy widow's veil.' In the cemetery itself there were estimated to be 10,000 people. It was as though a circus had come to town.

When the painful ceremony was over – against an aural background of 'Liz! Liz! Come out Liz!' from the crowd – Elizabeth tried to escape by car, but the gawping sightseers were all over it. For ten minutes the car was stuck there, beneath a heaving mound of people all peering in. Afterwards she said, 'People don't behave like that. But they do.'

After that experience there was sedation for a time, to numb the shock of loss, but that could not go on for ever. 'Round the bend' was not a route that Elizabeth intended to take, although it was a phrase that she used herself. Work itself would be the best therapy, she realized, so she went back to dramatic labour in *Cat on a Hot Tin Roof*. And, who knows, but the deep sadness and conflict within her after Todd's death might not have been a help in establishing the character of Maggie the Cat in what some think of as one of her finest performances?

The film is fine melodrama, with burning sexual undertones. In the Deep South family, dominated by Big Daddy (Burl Ives), the fact that he is dying of cancer is the cause of bitter battles over who will inherit. His favourite son (Paul Newman) is married to Maggie, but all they can do is bicker and quarrel because of his sexual inadequacy. The rest of the family tries to put itself in the way of the old man's favours. But Maggie is going to do her best finally to cure and bring to reality the husband she loves; she realizes that he is wanting, because of his inability to grow up and away from the atmosphere of Big Daddy.

It was a trying, wearing role for Elizabeth because so much of the talk, especially around Big Daddy, was about death; reminders of her recent loss were, therefore, all too apparent. But the cast was more than understanding about what she must have been going through, while director Richard Brooks was as tactful and understanding; she described him as a directorial dream. She had trouble, stuttering her lines at first, and could not say anything apart from popcorn – salted. But Brooks's patience with her overcame the first, while Burl Ives's conspiratorial kindness helped the second.

There was a scene in *Cat* in which she had to wolf down food. Usually, food on the set is fly-sprayed and left all day under the

When Liz played Maggie the Cat in *Cat on a Hot Tin Roof* (MGM) she was suffering from the devastating loss of Mike Todd. Her role was a wearing one, involving many harangues with Paul Newman.

lights. Burl Ives persuaded the prop boys to keep replenishing her plate with newly-baked ham and corn bread. That roused her appetite and they kept shooting the scene over and over again: 'Each time I ate and ate and ate.'

The film went into post-production trauma and Elizabeth decided that she, although brought up as a Christian Scientist, needed another religion. Why not the Jewish faith of her late husband? She felt she needed something which, she said to herself, was 'more formalized'. So, over the gestation period of nine months, she studied, and eventually was accepted into, the Reform branch of the faith. Her Jewish name: Elisheba Rachel. And it was a belonging that undoubtedly helped her face her worry when Liza, the child of herself and Mike Todd, fell victim to double pneumonia and nearly passed away. If she had died, Elizabeth wrote later, 'I don't think I could have borne that.'

What she was to bear, in fact, was the role that public opinion and the newspapers were to cast her in during another emotional involvement that was to be played out in the arena of world-wide gawping. Her role was to be that of Other Woman, and indiscretion was to be the better part of amour.

Eddie Fisher was a singer who occasionally made movies; Debbie Reynolds was a film actress who sometimes sang. Both had been married to the other for some time and, if anyone had a right to be known as America's Sweethearts, it was probably them. They seemed made for each other. They gave interviews to fan magazines in which they told how much each was made for the other, how much they loved each other. They were the Tony Curtis and Janet Leigh of their time. In private, though, things were not at all well, despite the supposedly healing bond of children. Fisher was therefore vulnerable to another kind of love, because of this private estrangement; Elizabeth was just as vulnerable because Todd's death had left her open and accessible.

Fisher had been a great friend of Todd's, openly admiring the man's life-style and his panache: this was something for the withdrawn Fisher to emulate and try to approach. He had been at Todd's funeral. It was only natural that he should try to comfort the widow. Not, though, according to the columnists and the gossips; not according to the

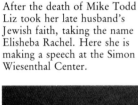

After the death of Mike Todd Liz took her late husband's Jewish faith, taking the name Elisheba Rachel. Here she is making a speech at the Simon Wiesenthal Center.

Left: There was bad publicity
for Elizabeth Taylor when
Eddie Fisher, Mike Todd's
friend, took much time and
trouble to comfort her after
Todd's death. Fisher was
supposedly ideally married to
Debbie Reynolds.

headlines which began to see Elizabeth as
greedy for another woman's husband.

It may have been because of the honesty
of their meetings that the friendship was so
criticized. Words such as 'home breaker'
were uttered loud and clear. She had a com-
mitment to make *Suddenly Last Summer*,
again by Tennessee Williams, but lingeringly
over that summer of 1959 the whole business
spluttered into suspect flame, fanned by
moralists declaiming in the newspapers. The
Fisher-Taylor affair was big news and those
concerned held Press conferences to put their
points of view, to point the sides that should
be taken. Which didn't help much either.
There was a lot of heat generated, but precious little illumination.

A divorce was asked for from Debbie Reynolds and there was much prevarication on
that score. Eventually it was agreed that it
might be better if the trio split the way that
Eddie Fisher and Elizabeth Taylor had
hoped for. Debbie Reynolds agreed to a
divorce.

Elizabeth and Fisher were married on 12
May 1960 at the Temple Betho Sholom in
Las Vegas. Elizabeth refused to listen to
those who said that Fisher was too like her
first two husbands, without the strength of
Mike Todd. She knew best. She later wrote:
'Maybe with Eddie I was trying to see if I
was alive or dead. Also, for some idiotic
reason I thought that Eddie needed me and
I should make *somebody* happy.'

They started out with the hope of happi-
ness shared by all newly-weds. Hopes for
Suddenly Last Summer were, however, running low. 'You mustn't do it, it's too raw,'
she was told. But she had a feel for it; des-

perately wanted to play the girl whose cousin's mother wants her lobotomized by
surgeon Montgomery Clift, because of her
memories of how cousin Sebastian died during that oppressive previous summer. That
cousin's mother was played by Katharine
Hepburn, who had previously looked
through Elizabeth when, as a youngster, she
had asked for an autograph. She no longer
looked through her now, for as the director
Joseph L. Mankiewicz said: 'Elizabeth is
close to being the greatest actress in the
world, and so far she has done it mostly by
instinct.'

The film was greeted with a mixture of
praise and blame; its combination of covert

Liz in *Suddenly Last Summer*
(Columbia), as a girl whose
aunt, Katharine Hepburn,
wants her lobotomized by
surgeon Montgomery Clift.

incest and homosexuality, allied to overt cannibalism, was a strange, provocative dish to set before the public. But it was for Elizabeth a personal triumph. As the girl fighting for her sanity and trying to keep a finger-grasp on a reality which threatens her mind, she is completely convincing as somebody who is triumphing through sheer will-power. It was a weird, baroque story and, certainly, Montgomery Clift did not appear to his best advantage in it. But it still works compulsively. It was something that Elizabeth had wanted to do – and had now done.

Something she did not want to do, but which MGM ordered her to do, was her next film, *Butterfield 8*. She had thought she was no longer at the studio's beck and call because of a verbal agreement with Mike Todd, but his death seemed to inspire what she bitterly called 'their usual gallantry'. She decided to make the best of a bad job.

Butterfield 8, from a story by John O'Hara, was not all that bad a job, but Elizabeth rebelled at the script which she thought of as 'pornographic', and not all that good, anyway. She was to play a nymphomaniac socialite caught up with a somewhat innocent Laurence Harvey. She went through the motions – which were for her to give of her best. And it is a film that can still, despite its inherent banality, catch the throat – especially in the sensitivity and despair glimpsed in Elizabeth's structuring of the character.

Finally, *Butterfield 8* was over and Elizabeth sat back to contemplate her future. There had been discussions of an epic in which she was to have been involved, but there had been little talk about it recently. It was causing a lot of trouble over at Twentieth Century-Fox, where a lot of money had already been spent on preparing it. So the call that came from producer Walter Wanger was not altogether unexpected.

He would like to talk some more about her appearing as *Cleopatra*. Rex Harrison was likely to be in it with another British actor. You know: Richard Burton.

EGYPTIAN LOVE SONG

Elizabeth sitting at the feet of the Sphinx for *Cleopatra* (Twentieth Century-Fox). The film became a legend for the length of time it took to make, and the tremendous costs which mounted to an astronomical level over the years.

There were, for several months after the shooting of *Cleopatra* had moved from England, occasions when visitors to the Pinewood Film Studios just outside London, would be invited to 'come and look at the ruins'. A few minutes walk to the back lot of one of the largest studios in England and there would be a sight to behold: one huge sphinx badly in need of repair, a couple of pyramids looking somewhat dishevelled, several items of Egyptiana. An English drizzle did not help the general air of bleak abandon; artefacts associated with the hot and dusty desert looked soddenly deserted and uninspiring.

This was all there was left, in England at any rate, of one of the costliest, most grandiloquent errors in film-making. Spyros Skouras, boss of Twentieth Century-Fox, who had been caught up in the whole enterprise from 1958, once said at some hysterical point of no-return: 'I don't know how I got on this band-wagon, but once on it's hard to get off.'

It had started in that year of 1958 with the idea of an enormous epic which would help Fox out of the doldrums in which its fortunes seemed to have stuck. Scripts were prepared, then dropped, in efforts to delineate, with cinematic effect, the story of the queen-goddess of Egypt and her love affairs, first with Caesar and then with Antony – a tragic decline which led to her clasping that asp to her bosom as a one-way ticket to the hereafter. Brigitte Bardot, then Susan Hayward, had been talked of as Cleopatra; somehow, though, it was always Elizabeth who was the inevitable choice, even though when producer Walter Wanger rang her about the proposition she asked for a million dollars – a monetary bracket hitherto unheard of.

Filming started in England, stopped, and started again. Now it was Rex Harrison who was to play Caesar and Richard Burton, wild young hope of the British stage latterly making a name in films, who was to play Antony. Director Rouben Mamoulian, who had worked on the project for some months, finally left, and Joseph L. Mankiewicz took over the jerky reins of control.

Mankiewicz was one of the more articulate and literary of Hollywood directors; he had thought through the character of Cleopatra and her love affairs. For her, he was quoted as saying, 'Politics gave way to passion; that was her undoing.' About Antony he said: 'He stood always in Caesar's footsteps – right up to and into Cleopatra's bed . . . his love for Cleopatra was, in the beginning, as guilt-ridden and frightened as that of a son in love with his father's mistress.' Mankiewicz's task was to save the picture and all the money that had been pumped into it.

Elizabeth, though, was in no mood for saving anything, of no mind to conjecture about the character of the complex woman she was to interpret. Living at the Dorchester Hotel in London with Eddie Fisher she was aware only too urgently that she had contracted Asian flu, a particularly virulent strain, which was why she spent her 29th birthday with a temperature so high it seemed to be going through the roof. The illness deepened into pneumonia; a private nurse was in attendance because Elizabeth so hated being in hospitals.

Then, making a routine check, the nurse realized that her patient had turned blue, that her nails were starting to blacken – and that she had stopped breathing. Elizabeth Taylor was suffocating to death.

The nurse phoned for a doctor and the hotel telephone operator knew there was a party being given at the Dorchester for a young medical student who was to be married. There were bound to be doctors there! There were. One of them, J. Middleton Price, was one of London's leading anaesthetists, who came bounding down the corridor in his evening dress. He dragged Elizabeth up by the heels to try to make her vomit up the congestion; he pounded at her, gouging at her eye knowing that the pain might make her come through the ever-enveloping coma. At last it happened: Elizabeth took her first deep breath – 'and then went crash out again for six days.'

The headlines tolled the news each day: about the tracheotomy that was performed and how her lungs were scoured of the gath-

ering mucus; how the Queen's doctor had been called in; how she was in an iron lung. The London Clinic, wherein she was being treated, was besieged by reporters. Letters poured in – missives of sympathy and adoration. The Scarlet Woman had, because of her illness, become The Martyred Lady.

Elizabeth wrote later, 'I just let the disease take me.' She kept thinking she had died, kept dreaming that she was talking with Mike Todd. Then all hallucinations faded. Weakly she looked up at the figures around her and knew that she was getting better: 'It was like being given sight, hearing, touch, sense of colour.'

Convalescing, she was to be given one more thing to speed her progress to health. She won the Oscar for her role in *Butterfield 8*. She was modest enough to say it was because she had nearly died of pneumonia, that it was 'a sympathy award'. Her leg was hugely bandaged for the ceremony, because where she had been fed intravenously had become infected: it looked very dramatic. But her gratitude for the Academy Award was still genuine: tears shone in her eyes and her voice when she spoke her speech of gratitude was constricted with emotion.

Then followed a summer of quietly contented recuperation, during which she discovered her children anew. In September 1961 shooting began again in Rome and Elizabeth was plunged into coming face to face with the Serpent of the Nile and an off-screen love affair with Richard Burton which was to ignite the flames of some of the fiercest controversy of her life.

Elizabeth was, on and off, connected with *Cleopatra* for around five years. It was a story, that production, of drama and intrigue worth filming for itself. Millions were spent on bringing forth a film for a world which must, at the end, have been rather tired of the whole enterprise. What they were not tired of, though, was the love of Richard Burton for Elizabeth Taylor.

Burton was born Richard Jenkins in South Wales, the twelfth of 13 children. His scholastic brilliance took the interest of teachers Meredith Jones and Philip Burton. He won a scholarship to Oxford University and there realized that acting was to be his life. He was married to Sybil Burton and they had two daughters. He had made a glowing name on the English stage, having learned, as he put it, 'so much from Sir John Gielgud'.

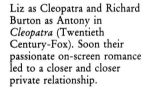

Liz as Cleopatra and Richard Burton as Antony in *Cleopatra* (Twentieth Century-Fox). Soon their passionate on-screen romance led to a closer and closer private relationship.

In Hollywood he had begun with *The Robe* and done other movies for Fox, but Spyros Skouras was not happy with him for the role of Antony. Not only was he reputed to be 'a wild one,' but did he have a real interest in the role?

He had, though, made a huge success as King Arthur in the musical *Camelot* on Broadway, and both Walter Wanger and Joseph L. Mankiewicz believed in him. He got the part. The newspapers reported that his price was to be 250,000 dollars over three

months. It was also reported that Elizabeth was not getting the million dollars she had asked for, but three-quarters of that amount. But the cost of such a price is the kind of fame that is expected to be available to the public every minute of every day. Burton later said: 'I had not realized that she was so famous, that everything that she did would be noted as though it already had a legendary quality.'

Her impression of him at first was that 'he was rather full of himself'. But she invited

Rex Harrison was Caesar to Liz's Cleopatra in *Cleopatra* (Twentieth Century-Fox). The film never lived up to its multi-million dollar investment.

Liz with Eddie Fisher. They married in 1960, after Debbie Reynolds had agreed to a divorce. However, Liz began filming with Richard Burton in 1961, and her love life was once again in the news.

Far right: Liz and Burton. Their marriages, splits, reconciliations and his immensely expensive presents of jewellery to her made them the most publicized couple in the world.

him to talk, envied him being a 'genuine actor and not a movie star'. His seeming vanity may well have been because he was in some awe of her. She warmed to him on the first day they were to work together, when she saw that he was only too human: 'I've never seen a gentleman so hung over in my whole life. He was kind of quivering from head to foot and there were grog blossoms – you know, from booze – all over his face.' Coffee stilled his trembling, but he still fluffed a line. That vulnerability won her heart.

That heart was a very public affair, as had been proved so often in the past. Perhaps Burton did not, as has been said, know what he was getting into; Elizabeth may have known, but her judgement was blurred by love. Mankiewicz eventually told Wanger: 'They are not just playing Antony and Cleopatra.' The photographers along the Via Veneto could have told him weeks before.

One of the qualities that Burton always admired about Elizabeth was her courage, 'her sheer bloody guts'. That approval grew from incidents such as he having to hit her on set, so that she fell on the so-fragile back. That she managed it was the occasion for applause. More applause, too, for the fact that the film was grinding to a conclusion; arguments there may have been – Rex Harrison shouting for a Cadillac because Elizabeth had one was one story – but the film was about to be finally over.

There is an anecdote that, while filming in Alexandria for some desert shots, Mankiewicz was observed being carried on a stretcher with a pen and a sheet of paper in his hand. 'I'm writing the last scene,' he called weakly. The last scene, though, of the Burton-Taylor romance was not by any means written, despite the fact that others were commenting on it. The Vatican itself, and supposedly the Holy See, said of this unholy sight: 'These are the caprices of adult children.' It was the most publicized and public romance possibly ever conducted. There was further comment in the Vatican City weekly paper, *L'Osser-*

54

Above: Richard Burton and Liz in the early stages of their relationship. This is *Cleopatra* (Twentieth Century-Fox).

Right: The young Burton with Victor Mature in the first Cinemascope film, *The Robe* (Twentieth Century-Fox), in 1953. He was not impressive and Fox's Spyros Skouras was against his casting as Antony in *Cleopatra*.

vatore della Dominica, which attacked her as a mother. 'The housewife and the bricklayer would have worked harder and would have seriously made sacrifices for their child. You, instead, have other things to do.'

In *Cleopatra* there is a scene of extravagant spectacle as the queen enters Rome. It is an enormous affair with Elizabeth perched high on a massive, mobile sphinx, while extras mill around below her. It was symbolic of the eminence she had achieved as a superstar: a lonely, impossible height, the further from which to fall. '*Le scandale*' seemed about to bring her down in the world's favour.

Hume Cronyn, the actor, took advantage of the ending of the movie to shout 'Hallelujah' and leap overboard from the queen's barge. 'It's so good!' he shouted from the water. What had been good between Elizabeth and Burton now seemed to be over. Both went back to their respective hideaways in Switzerland. And the world waited: how long could, how long would, such a separation last?

GONE FOR A BURTON

Elizabeth had written a letter to Burton saying that she thought their love was destroying too many lives around them. There was no response from him. Then they sat tight in their Swiss homes – he in Geneva, she at Gstaad. They licked their separate wounds, reading the newspapers which still persisted in writing about them, and feeling angry because Joseph L. Mankiewicz had been taken off the editing of *Cleopatra* by the new power at Fox, Darryl F. Zanuck. The cutting of a film is, obviously, very important to such an endeavour, especially one that had gone on so long and with so many complications as *Cleopatra*. What Zanuck did to *Cleopatra*, when Mankiewicz was no longer around and in control, is said, by some, to account for what was wrong with the movie when it was finally screened. Certainly, it looked as though the role of Antony had suffered in the editing 'committed' by Zanuck.

So the two of them held their peace. Then one day came a letter from Burton suggesting luncheon. 'I had sincerely thought I would never see him again,' she recalls. And they met at the Château de Chillon at Lake Geneva at two o'clock. They met, after that, about every three weeks or so; then the meetings accelerated. It was a force that both found irresistible. And the newspapers had a fresh target in the two of them. There was more gossip about her maternal duties – she had adopted another little girl, Maria, to add to her family – but they seemed aware of how important it was to ignore such snide remarks.

There was one legitimate way for them to be together – and that was in a film. And there was a script around for which other stars had been suggested. As two of the most romantic Very Important Persons of the time it seemed natural that they should star in *The V.I.P.s*. This was scripted by the British playwright Terence Rattigan, and was lush glossy nonsense about fog-bound passengers of some rank and degree caught at London's Heathrow Airport. Burton and Elizabeth were a husband and wife who, only finally, realize that they need each other; she's about

to leave him with another man. But how could Richard Burton and Elizabeth Taylor ever be separated? They were as Laurel and Hardy: a legendary twosome, a pair that had become, as somebody pointed out, The Royal Couple of Romance.

Burton followed that film with Tennessee Williams' *The Night of the Iguana*, which director John Huston was shooting in Mexico. Huston has written: 'The tangled web of relationships among the *Night of the Iguana* principals set something of a record.

A happy-looking Liz in *The V.I.P.s* (MGM), in which she and Burton played together as husband and wife. She thinks of leaving him but they come together at the end – for a long time almost perfect type-casting.

57

Taylor and Burton together in *The V.I.P.s* (MGM), which was released in 1963. When making the film, both were married. It was not until 1964 that they were both free.

Richard Burton was accompanied by Elizabeth Taylor, who was still married to Eddie Fisher. Michael Wilding, Elizabeth's ex-husband, arrived to handle the job of publicizing Richard Burton. . .'

The film also starred Ava Gardner, who had her own problems, Deborah Kerr and Sue Lyons. Huston bought five gold-plated derringers which he solemnly presented all round. Each gun had four golden bullets engraved with the names of the other stars. As it was 'All the members of the cast – especially our stars – got along famously.'

Burton's marriage ended towards the end of 1963, but Elizabeth had to wait for some months until her own marriage was dis-

solved. Eddie Fisher's much-publicized acrimony was one of the reasons for the delay. Burton was reported to have asked Fisher to 'do the gentlemanly thing'. To which Fisher had responded by saying: 'He should stick by his Shakespearian roles.' But in March the legal restriction was lifted, and Burton and Elizabeth Taylor were married in Montreal in Canada, where Burton was appearing in *Hamlet*.

Laurence Olivier once spoke about the impertinence he and Vivien Leigh, who was not then his wife, had shown in appearing together in *Romeo and Juliet* in New York. 'It was as though we were asking the public to endorse our relationship. No wonder it

Left: Liz and Burton returning to Toronto the day after their secret marriage in Montreal. Burton had to get back for a pre-Broadway run of 'Hamlet'.

Below: The happy couple are obviously in very good spirits as they answer reporters' questions. Few pairs have been interviewed so often in the last few years.

Right: In *The Sandpiper* (MGM), Liz was a beatnik who fell for Burton, but despite the passion the film was disappointing.

Far right, above: A dishevelled Liz in *Who's Afraid of Virginia Woolf?* (Warner Bros.), in which the stormy relationship she enjoyed with Burton off-screen was mirrored to some extent to make an explosive film.

Far right, below: College professor Burton and his wife, Elizabeth Taylor, fight and argue incessantly in *Who's Afraid of Virginia Woolf?* (Warner Bros.), much to the embarrassment of young guests George Segal and Sandy Dennis.

was all a disaster; the public seemed to realize that it was being conned.' Burton and Elizabeth had been doing very much the same thing, but on world-wide scale, as a slightly older Romeo and Juliet, and the public had reacted unfavourably. But now they were married and a lot of the gossip fell away: the public endorsed them as characters to be treasured. And Elizabeth and Burton went along with that, as who wouldn't?

They were a remarkable, splendid combination, often making remarks in interviews reported in newspapers and on television which sounded outrageous. Burton talked about Elizabeth bringing him repose, especially at night; Elizabeth said he made her feel so intelligent – 'and, of course, I'm not at all.' It was as though the long months of *le scandale* had convinced them that this was the way to behave, even though married. As

though, 'If these are the roles you want us to play – then we'll play them.'

In 1964 they made one film together, *The Sandpiper*, which was the kind of tear-logged romance which, despite what others have said, showed that Elizabeth's eye for a good script could err. It cast her as a beatnik who falls in love with an upright Burton, who is married to Eva Marie-Saint. The Big Sur locations helped, but not much. But next year came a movie that was to establish them as a couple who could use their own relationship in the most dramatic ways possible to conjure a compulsive magic out of the material. The film: *Who's Afraid of Virginia Woolf?*

Adapted from the play by Edward Albee, and directed by Mike Nichols, it tells of the corrosive bitterness between an ageing college professor (Burton) and his bitching wife

(Elizabeth). A younger couple – George Segal and Sandy Dennis – are invited home for drinks; they watch as the older pair seem to delight in tearing each other to pieces. It was a film whose language caused some consternation because of its sexual frankness, but certainly it drew from both of them performances that have a haunted bitterness and, strangely, love. With this Elizabeth collected her second Oscar for best actress; she went round for days afterwards saying that Burton should have had an Oscar, too.

The self-critical Burton said of his role, 'My prime concern is that my quality is not exactly this, an American college professor going to seed.' He went to see it again and commented, 'I wanted to kill myself, because I thought I was so indifferent. Not bad, indifferent.' Elizabeth knew that he had given a great performance, as he had. Later he told

an interviewer that by marrying her he had become a far more important actor.

As a duet they still sang close harmony, although it was hard to hear it sometimes, because of the confusion of sound around them: they had an incredible entourage, from publicists to secretaries, from bodyguards to baby-minders. 'They carry their own tribe around with them,' wrote one journalist. 'It's as though Burton were making up for his family in Wales.'

Their choice of movies which they thought they could do together was not always to be as advantageous as *Virginia Woolf? Dr Faustus* by Marlowe – which she played as a non-speaking Helen of Troy – and, much later, Dylan Thomas' *Under Milk Wood*, just did not work. More successful was Shakespeare's *The Taming of the Shrew*, which was directed by Franco Zeffirelli, with Elizabeth as a betwitching, humorous Kate. Their difficulty always in representing other characters was in shaking off the personae of Burton and Taylor. Burton said, 'We are an institution, God help us.'

The Comedians, from a political novel by Graham Greene, was a brave attempt to record what was happening so brutally in Haiti, but it only succeeded in disturbing its audience. Elizabeth's accent for the part was

Above: Liz made a series of films with Burton in the early 1970s. This is *Under Milk Wood* (Altura Films), with Liz holding the bottle for Peter O'Toole.

Right: Burton and Taylor once again playing a warring couple, this time in Shakespeare. *The Taming of the Shrew* (Columbia) was a good and successful film.

Far right: Was this the face that launched a thousand ships? Liz as Helen of Troy in *Dr Faustus* (Columbia) in which Burton directed and starred with her.

Right: Liz and Burton arriving at Heathrow Airport from Geneva in 1967. With them are Michael and Christopher, Liz's sons from her marriage with Michael Wilding.

Far right: With The Master. Noel Coward had a part in *Boom*! (Universal), a Tennessee Williams story which was shot in Sardinia. Liz was a rich woman facing death.

unconvincing and Burton's hero was of such a doleful countenance that no audience could identify with his worries. Their next movie was of another alienating narrative: *Boom*!, a version of Tennessee Williams' (again) 'The Milk Train Doesn't Stop Here Anymore'. This had Elizabeth as The Richest Woman in the Universe slowly dying on a small Mediterranean island. It was shot in Sardinia and looks stunning even if its theme – with Burton coming in late as a kind of Angel of Death – was not the most engaging. Joseph Losey directed to some baroque effect. It was not effective enough, however.

Now was the time for the bizarre. While Burton went off to make a Boy's Own Paper story, *Where Eagles Dare*, Elizabeth and Mia Farrow were making *Secret Ceremony* with Robert Mitchum. Parentless heiress (Farrow) meets a woman (Elizabeth) whom she discovers has been a prostitute. Mia Farrow 'adopts' her as a 'mother' but maternal affection sours into rivalry and bitterness. Losey directed this one, too, which may explain something. Losey is a brilliant film-maker who has to be prevented almost physically from going over the top. Nobody seemed to try very hard to do that on *Secret Ceremony*.

Right: Graham Greene wrote the book for *The Comedians* (MGM). As well as Liz, the strong cast included Alec Guinness.

Far right: *The Only Game in Town* (Twentieth Century-Fox) was craps. Liz at the table with co-star Warren Beatty.

Below: *Secret Ceremony* (Universal) was an undistinguished film in which a rich heiress, Mia Farrow, befriends prostitute Liz, but no good comes of it.

Above: Elizabeth Taylor shot *The Only Game in Town* in Boulogne and was reunited on set with her two daughters who were on holiday from school in Switzerland – Maria Burton, six (front), and Liza Todd, eleven.

Far right: Another family picture – Liz on the beach with her sons Michael Wilding and Christopher Wilding and daughter Liza Todd.

More convincing was *The Only Game in Town*, in which Elizabeth was reunited with George Stevens as the chorus girl to Warren Beatty's gambler. It was a simple enough romance, of which Stevens remarked bitterly in terms of the way movies were becoming more violent, 'it might be ahead of its time.' It is a film with a lot of tenderness, but he judged the public mood aright.

It was in 1969, just after *The Only Game in Town*, that Elizabeth had another operation: her uterus was removed. Her strength of will triumphed over her body's weakness and she managed to joke, 'God knows how many this has been.' The next film of any note was *X, Y and Zee* (called *Zee and Company* in Great Britain) from a story by the novelist Edna O'Brien, with Elizabeth as Michael Caine's bawdy wife fighting for him over the soon-to-be recumbent body of his mistress, Susannah York. It was not so much convincing as convicted by its lack of real credibility in concept. Worse was to follow with *Hammersmith is Out*, in which Burton and she were re-united: he as a wild criminal who keeps breaking out of prison trying to sire a son. She is one who helps him try.

Night Watch, with a terminally ill Laurence Harvey, followed. As a thriller it just did not know how to thrill, although it can be forgiven because so many accidents happened on it, including Elizabeth breaking her

Another turbulent on-screen relationship for Liz in *X, Y and Zee* (*Zee and Company* in Britain) was as the wife of Michael Caine.

The man in the background on the set of *Divorce His; Divorce Hers* looks alert. He was Liz's bodyguard appointed after threats from Black September terrorists arising from her adoption of the Jewish faith.

finger. Then came the disastrous *Divorce His; Divorce Hers*. Banal to the point of being ridiculous, it had been an intriguing idea: divorce seen through the eyes of the protagonists.

Over the next months there were *Ash Wednesday* and *The Driver's Seat*; neither of any note and neither nearly as dramatic as the love between Richard Burton and she which underneath all this was shuddering to a halt. Was it the drinking? He made several public confessions of the amount of alcohol he had needed to get through a day, but she had known all about that already. Their oft-reported remarks about each other now stung like bullets. There had been rumours for some time: two separations and two re-unions. Burton said, 'It wasn't drink. It was career.'

Either way, Elizabeth felt that she had tried hard enough. It had lasted ten years. *Divorce His; Divorce Hers* turned out to be a prophetic title. For Liz, divorce became a cold, bitter reality once again.

REFLECTIONS IN VIOLET EYES

Habit dies hard. Elizabeth and Burton had been fused together for so long that their familiarity had become entirely precious to them; they could not imagine being separated, even now. And so, incredibly, they re-married in 1975 in the African country of Botswana, which seemed some sort of neutral territory. Burton announced that he was going to give her a million-dollar diamond to add to her already large and famous collection of jewellery. The world's Press was there, of course, but even on this new wedding day it was noted that Burton was drinking again. It was a remarriage that barely lasted a few weeks; a gesture at reconciliation that failed. Then Elizabeth was alone again.

There were always films to occupy her life, but not so many now. Or perhaps it was that Elizabeth no longer felt the need for them; that there were few of the kind of movies around that she felt happiest in. *The Blue Bird* was one that she tried. This was a co-production by Twentieth Century-Fox with the Soviet Union, and was made there by director George Cukor. That was in 1976. It was premiered, but has never been generally released. All that is known is that it is taken from the famous fantasy by Maurice Maeterlinck. Perhaps some day it will be shown and we can see if it measures up to her reputation – or not.

Certainly her reputation was not helped by *Victory at Entebbe*, which was also made in 1976. This was assembled quickly after the Israeli raid to rescue hostages who were being held inside General Amin's Uganda, and shows only too obviously the haste with which it was put together. Elizabeth played a Jewish woman, desperate for news of what is happening to the hostages, and at least makes some brave show of a role which was not at all well conceived or carried through. There was a universal thumbs-down from the critics. After which movie another: an adaptation of the Stephen Sondheim musical, *A Little Night Music*, which like *The Blue Bird* seems to have been consigned to oblivion.

In 1980 Elizabeth returned to England to make an oh-so-English crime thriller, based

on an Agatha Christie story, *The Mirror Crack'd*. It was an expensive piece of flimsy, following in the successful wake of other Christie movies such as *Murder on the Orient Express* and *Death on the Nile*. This did not have the pulling power as those others, perhaps because there were no out-of-the-way locations, but simply a Mummersetshire village as the centre of activities.

Another arrival at another airport after another marriage to Richard Burton. This was Heathrow after the 1975 wedding in Botswana.

Far right: Two mature love goddesses of the screen. Liz with Ava Gardner in *The Blue Bird* (Twentieth Century-Fox), made in the Soviet Union, and not generally released.

Here are gathered the various exotic members of a film unit on location, to film Elizabeth playing a film star making a come-back after a nervous breakdown. Husband Rock Hudson tries to smooth a way for her, but co-star Kim Novak is much given to slanging her rival, while producer Tony Curtis looks on.

The killing of a village housewife is interleaved into the not-very-convincing mimickry, but Elizabeth was, in fact, very good as the character who had no real rhyme or reason – until the predictable twist in the ending revealed all. She made it seem to work, as director Guy Hamilton was the first to admit, while Miss Novak was notably generous about the generosity of Elizabeth on camera. 'She'll let you take a scene away from her, if she thinks it would help the scene.'

That's the cinematic progress of Elizabeth Taylor to the early 1980s. Her progress in

other directions has managed to surprise even those who thought they were beyond such an emotion in contemplation of her career. Her marriage to John Warner, a former high-up government official, showed her moving into areas of politics which surprised even her. But, by all accounts, she always backed him at functions and generally was the most charismatic politician's wife around. Then in 1981 she went on stage for the first time, for a long-running performance in a revival of Lillian Hellman's 'The Little Foxes', in the raw-and-meaty role of the ruthless Regina. It was a performance that divided critics as to her stage presence, but all agreed that hers was the most remarkable and dominating personality on that stage. As on screen.

For even her fiercest critics admit that whatever the cinematic context, however awful the product – and her taste has never always been of the best in this connection –

Below: Liz with Harold Prince in *A Little Night Music* (New World), another recent film which seems to have vanished into limbo.

there is something in Elizabeth Taylor that *communicates*. Take *Reflections in a Golden Eye* (1967) in which she starred with Marlon Brando. The location is an American Army post and Brando is a latent homosexual major who is constantly ridiculed by his brainless, weak wife (Elizabeth). From a novel by Carson McCullers, the screen is filled with grotesques of one kind or another. Brando's is a marvellous performance, but it is Elizabeth whom we remember, for what she communicates of this infantile woman. She convinces us that we should show compassion for this creature who does not understand herself, let alone her strange husband. It could have been a vast, showy role, full of flaunting rhetoric. But Elizabeth scales it down so that the grotesquerie can be perceived on our human level. Even in her worst films there is always something, even if it's only a fragment, that communicates with us, the audience . . .that convinces us.

The director John Huston believes *Reflections in a Golden Eye* to be one of his best pictures and admired Elizabeth, he says, not only for managing to ride a white stallion despite ever-increasing back pains, but because 'I discovered that, more than a great beauty and a personality, she was a supremely fine actress.' After the filming he and producer Ray Stark sent her an ivory horse set in gold as a remembrance of reflections past.

Elizabeth's jewellery, too, has always made the headlines. There was, it seemed, never to be a day go by during her marriage to Richard Burton, when there was not a story about him giving her some exquisite gem or other – from the platinum wedding ring with which he wed her (the first time) to the twenty-dollar gold piece surrounded by rubies on their tenth anniversary. One of the most famous presents was a heart-shaped diamond pendant of Indian antiquity estimated to cost nearly 100,000 dollars.

In a way, of course, they might be regarded as Crown Jewels, for Elizabeth has become a queen of a kind, as much for her staying power as for the regal aura which now emanates from her. At the last count

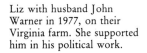

Liz with husband John Warner in 1977, on their Virginia farm. She supported him in his political work.

Above: Liz in the 1980s,
starring in *The Mirror Crack'd*
(EMI Films). She plays one of
a pair of feuding film stars –
Kim Novak (left) is the other,
and Rock Hudson and Tony
Curtis their husbands.

Left: In *Reflections in a
Golden Eye* (Warner Bros.)
Liz plays cards with Brian
Keith while her homosexual
husband, Marlon Brando,
sulks in the background.

75

Above: Liz looking as glamorous as ever on stage at the Martin Beck Theater in 1981 with Maureen Stapleton, in the production of Lillian Hellmann's 'The Little Foxes'.

Right: A happy picture of Liz at a party thrown for her 40th birthday.

she had made 54 films, which makes many other film stars seem remarkably ephemeral: she's the shining light to their flashes in the pan. 'I'm a survivor,' she says. It is said with some degree of modesty as to her real prowess but, in fact, to survive in the film business is a feat in itself: it shows a resilience which demands and commands respect.

If she turns up late on set, as she has been known to do, it is because, as John Huston says, 'she's a professional; she's not going to show her face before she's completely ready.' Director Waris Hussein, on *Divorce His; Divorce Hers*, asked her to blow her nose during one close-up. 'I have never blown my nose on film and I am not going to now,' she replied. There's a woman who knows exactly how she wants to come across.

She herself says, though, 'The Elizabeth Taylor who's famous, the one on celluloid, really has no depth or meaning to me. It's a totally superficial working thing, a commodity. . . . I really have never tried to analyze why so many people go to my movies. I

Far right: Elizabeth Taylor at 50. In London for her début on the English stage in *The Little Foxes*, she celebrated her birthday with a star-studded party at the Mayfair nightclub 'Legends' escorted by Richard Burton.

Right: A movie queen meets a real one. Liz Taylor and John Warner being introduced to the Queen.

suppose if people stopped buying the commodity and I cared, I would try to figure out what ingredients are missing.'

So what are the ingredients that are there? A rare beauty. An ability to suggest a kind of vulnerable, tender waywardness. A sense of who she is. She has survived as herself in a world where so much is done in public, in the glare of the spotlight, with an air of seeming tranquility. At the premiere of *The Blue Bird*, director George Cukor asked her how

she got through all the light-popping flashes of the scores of cameramen. 'I just wipe them away,' she said, and mimed wiping the lights from her face.

The lights are still there, though. For queens are always in the spotlight. And it is still a sign of her superstar quality that when next she appears we will still look and wonder. At her approach – the approach of Elizabeth Taylor – the public eye still widens in anticipation.

FILMOGRAPHY

There's One Born Every Minute. 1942. Universal. Director: Harold Young. With Hugh Herbert, Peggy Moran, Edgar Kennedy, Alfalfa Switzer.

Lassie Come Home. 1943. MGM. Director: Fred M. Wilcox. With Roddy McDowall, Donald Crisp, Edmund Gwenn, Dame May Whitty, Nigel Bruce.

Jane Eyre. 1944. Twentieth Century-Fox. Director: Robert Stevenson. With Orson Welles, Joan Fontaine, Margaret O'Brien, Peggy Anne Garner.

The White Cliffs of Dover. 1944. MGM. Director: Clarence Brown. With Irene Dunne, Alan Marshall, Frank Morgan, Dame May Whitty.

National Velvet. 1945. MGM. Director: Clarence Brown. With Mickey Rooney, Donald Crisp, Anne Revere, Angela Lansbury.

Courage of Lassie. 1946. MGM. Director: Fred Wilcox. With Frank Morgan, Tom Drake, Selena Royle, Harry Davenport.

Cynthia. 1947. MGM. Director: Robert Z. Leonard. With George Murphy, S. Z. Sakall, Mary Astor, Gene Lockhart.

Life with Father. 1947. Warner Bros. Director: Michael Curtiz. With William Powell, Irene Dunne, Edmund Gwenn.

A Date with Judy. 1948. MGM. Director: Richard Thorpe. With Wallace Beery, Jane Powell, Carmen Miranda, Xavier Cugat.

Julia Misbehaves. 1948. MGM. Director: Jack Conway. With Greer Garson, Walter Pidgeon, Peter Lawford, Cesar Romero.

Little Women. 1949. MGM. Director: Mervin LeRoy. With June Allyson, Peter Lawford, Margaret O'Brien, Janet Leigh, Rossano Brazzi.

Conspirator. 1950. MGM. Director: Victor Saville. With Robert Taylor, Robert Fleming, Harold Warrender, Honor Blackman.

The Big Hangover. 1950. MGM. Director: Norman Krasna. With Van Johnson.

Father of the Bride. 1950. MGM. Director: Vincente Minnelli. With Spencer Tracy, Joan Bennett, Don Taylor, Billie Burke, Leo G. Carroll.

Father's Little Dividend. 1951. MGM. Director: Vincente Minnelli. With Spencer Tracy, Joan Bennett, Don Taylor, Billie Burke.

A Place in the Sun. 1951. Paramount. Director: George Stevens. With Montgomery Clift, Shelley Winters, Anne Revere.

Callaway Went Thataway. 1951. MGM. Directors: Norman Panama and Melvin Frank. With Fred MacMurray, Dorothy McGuire, Howard Keel.

Love Is Better Than Ever. 1952. MGM. Director: Stanley Donen. With Larry Parks, Josephine Hutchinson, Tom Tully.

Ivanhoe. 1952. MGM. Director: Richard Thorpe. With Robert Taylor, Joan Fontaine, George Sanders.

The Girl Who Had Everything. 1953. MGM. Director: Richard Thorpe. With Fernando Lamas, William Powell, Gig Young.

Rhapsody. 1954. MGM. Director: Charles Vidor. With Vittorio Gassman, John Ericson, Louis Calhern.

Elephant Walk. 1954. Paramount. Director: William Dieterle. With Dana Andrews, Peter Finch, Abraham Sofaer.

Beau Brummell. 1954. MGM. Director: Curtis Bernhardt. With Stewart Granger, Peter Ustinov, Robert Morley, James Donald.

The Last Time I Saw Paris. 1954. MGM. Director: Richard Brooks. With Van Johnson, Walter Pidgeon, Donna Reed.

Giant. 1956. Warner Bros. Director: George Stevens. With Rock Hudson, James Dean, Carroll Baker, Jane Withers.

Raintree County. 1957. MGM. Director: Edward Dmytryk. With Montgomery Clift, Eva Marie Saint, Nigel Patrick.

Cat on a Hot Tin Roof. 1958. MGM. Director: Richard Brooks. With Paul Newman, Burl Ives, Jack Carson, Judith Anderson.

Suddenly, Last Summer. 1959. Columbia. Director: Joseph L. Mankiewicz. With Katharine Hepburn, Montgomery Clift, Albert Dekker.

Scent of Mystery. 1960. Michael Todd Jr. Director: Jack Cardiff. With Denholm Elliott, Peter Lorre.

Butterfield 8. 1960. MGM. Director: Daniel Mann. With Laurence Harvey, Eddie Fisher, Dina Merrill.

Cleopatra. 1963. Twentieth Century-Fox. Director: Joseph L. Mankiewicz. With Richard Burton, Rex Harrison, Pamela Brown.

The V.I.P.s. 1963. MGM. Director: Anthony Asquith. With Richard Burton, Louis Jourdan.

The Sandpiper. 1965. MGM. Director: Vincente Minnelli. With Richard Burton, Eva Marie Saint, Charles Bronson.

Who's Afraid of Virginia Woolf? 1966. Warner Bros. Director: Mike Nichols. With Richard Burton, George Segal, Sandy Dennis.

The Taming of the Shrew. 1967. Columbia. Director: Franco Zeffirelli. With Richard Burton, Cyril Cusack, Michael Hordern.

Dr Faustus. 1967. Columbia. Directors: Richard Burton, Nevill Coghill. With Richard Burton, Andreas Teuber.

Reflections in a Golden Eye. 1967. Warner Bros. Director: John Huston. With Marlon Brando, Brian Keith, Julie Harris.

The Comedians. 1967. MGM. Director: Peter Glenville. With Richard Burton, Alec Guinness, Peter Ustinov, Paul Ford.

Boom! 1968. Universal. Director: Joseph Losey. With Richard Burton, Noel Coward, Joanna Shimkus.

Secret Ceremony. 1968. Universal. Director: Joseph Losey. With Mia Farrow, Robert Mitchum.

The Only Game in Town. 1970. Twentieth Century-Fox. Director: George Stevens. With Warren Beatty.

Under Milk Wood. 1972. Altura Films. Director: Andrew Sinclair. With Richard Burton, Peter O'Toole, Glynis Johns, Vivien Merchant.

X, Y and Zee (in Great Britain *Zee and Company*). 1972. Columbia. Director: Brian Hutton. With Michael Caine, Susannah York, Margaret Leighton.

Hammersmith Is Out. 1972. J. Cornelius Crean Films. Director: Peter Ustinov. With Richard Burton, Peter Ustinov, Beau Bridges.

Divorce His; Divorce Hers. 1973. ABC-TV. Director: Waris Hussein. With Richard Burton.

Night Watch. 1973. Avco-Embassy. Director: Brian Hutton. With Laurence Harvey, Billie Whitelaw.

Ash Wednesday. 1973. Paramount. Director: Larry Peerce. With Henry Fonda, Helmut Berger.

That's Entertainment! 1974. MGM. Director: Jack Haley, Jr. With Fred Astaire, Bing Crosby, and many others.

The Driver's Seat. 1974. Avco-Embassy. Director: Giuseppe Patroni-Griffi. With Ian Bannen.

The Blue Bird. 1976. Twentieth Century-Fox. Director: George Cukor. With Jane Fonda, Cicely Tyson, Ava Gardner.

Victory at Entebbe. 1976. David L. Wolper Productions. Director: Marvin J. Chomsky. With Helmut Berger, Theodore Bikel.

A Little Night Music. 1977. New World. Director: Harold Prince. With Diana Rigg, Len Cariou.

Winter Kills. 1979. Avco-Embassy. Director: William Richert. With Jeff Bridges, John Huston.

The Mirror Crack'd. 1980. EMI Films. Director: Guy Hamilton. With Angela Lansbury, Wendy Morgan, Tony Curtis, Kim Novak, Rock Hudson.